JOHN

NCP Biblical Commentaries

Resources for Pastoral Ministry

General Editor
Mary-Ann Getty Sullivan

NCP's biblical commentaries present the best of contemporary exegetical and theological scholarship in a clear, readable, inclusive style. The series provides readers with resources to better understand and integrate scriptural teachings with their own personal, social, spiritual and ecclesial lives.

Each volume provides an introduction to one or more books of the Bible, including an overview of the time, place and circumstances of composition, and the main issues addressed by the sacred writers. The biblical text is accompanied by an exposition of the issues and questions it raises for readers. Further insights from the history of its interpretation and practical applications for its significance today follow.

The volumes in this series are designed for committed Christians — women and men interested in deepening their faith and understanding of the importance of the scriptures to their daily life. They also help readers develop a scriptural basis for their personal spirituality as well as their commitment to the ecclesial community of faith.

JOHN
STORIES OF THE WORD AND FAITH

ROBERT J. KARRIS

New City Press
Hyde Park, NY

Published in the United States by New City Press
202 Cardinal Rd., Hyde Park, NY 12538
©2008 Robert J. Karris

Cover design by Durva Correia

Library of Congress Cataloging-in-Publication Data:
Karris, Robert J.
    John : stories of the Word and faith / Robert J. Karris.
      p. cm. -- (NCP biblical commentaries)
    Includes bibliographical references and index.
    ISBN 978-1-56548-297-5 (pbk. : alk. paper)
    1. Bible. N.T. John--Commentaries. I. Title

    BS2615.53.K37 2008
    226.5'077--dc22   2008018235

Printed in the United States of America

Contents

Introduction

I write this commentary to nourish and deepen faith. This is not just my own perspective, but that of John himself who specified his purpose in the conclusion to his Gospel: "These things are written that you may believe and continue to believe that Jesus is the Messiah, the Son of God, and that through this belief you may have life in his name" (20:31 in author's translation). In each section of my commentary I will stress the dimension of faith, often in the final paragraph. I write primarily for those involved in pastoral ministry who want a commentary with solid content, but also with heart. To reach them, I write in plain language and use frequent illustrations and anecdotes.

Let John Be John

This commentary demands that you and I engage in disciplined reading. Put simply: We must let John be John. What do I mean? First, we can only discuss what the Gospel of John actually contains, not what we would like it to. John does not present Jesus as a babe in the manger and does not mention the magi paying homage to the newborn king of the Jews. John has no parable of the Good Samaritan, no parable of the Prodigal Son, no Parable of the Last

Judgment when the sheep and goats are separated on the basis of care of the needy. Further, John has no Sermon on the Mount, not even the shorter Sermon on the Plain. While Matthew, Mark, and Luke have Jesus going to Jerusalem just once during his public ministry, John has Jesus making that journey four times. Moreover, unlike the other three evangelists, John opens with a hymnic Prologue.

Second, to let John be John we can't reduce all the gospels to one. While each tells the story of Jesus' cleansing of the Temple, John is unique in placing this event not at the end of Jesus' ministry, but at its beginning. Each has at least one story of the multiplication of loaves, but only John explains its meaning with a lengthy discourse that follows. If we are going to allow John to be John, we can't combine these stories into one homogenized version. I think of a confrere who, due to an illness, has no sense of taste and a limited capacity to chew and swallow. Still, he has not lost his sense of humor. He'll banter with us as he puts a piece of ham, a couple of beets, a few carrots, and a red potato into a blender. Once he has created his gray concoction, he sits down with us and enjoys the drink and our company. While blending four different foods may nourish my confrere, blending Matthew, Mark, Luke, and John will not help us appreciate what is unique to John's Gospel. Let John be John!

Third, before reading this commentary, readers owe it to themselves to read the Gospel of John in one or two sittings. We must overcome the tendency to read John's Gospel without paying attention to context and narrative sequence. Those who only hear the gospel in bits and pieces at Sunday liturgies may never have had the experience that John intended. This commentary shows the interconnectedness of the various pericopes, or passages. For example, I underline that what Jesus predicted in his Farewell Discourse (Jn 13–17) comes true in his resurrection appearances (Jn 20–21). Indeed, let John be John.

Representative Characters

During the last three decades scholars have paid special attention to the characters in John's Gospel, for they are the springboards of faith. This commentary will highlight such "representative characters" or "representative figures." They stand for various believers or even individuals in various stages of their response to Jesus. Among the positive representative figures are the Samaritan woman, Martha and Mary, Mary of Magdala, Nicodemus, and the Beloved Disciple. Among the negative representative characters are Judas and Pilate. I liken the positive representative figures to the glorious tapestries that line sides of the nave of the Cathedral of Our Lady of the Angels in Los Angeles, some dedicated to unknown saints, adult men and women as well as girls and boys. I imagine that in the meeting places of the Johannine community similar tapestries must have honored its marginalized and nameless, cast aside as ignorant of the Law (see 7:49), as heroes and heroines.

Jesus and the Marginalized

For centuries John was labeled "the spiritual Gospel," as if the Word never became flesh like us in all things but sin. Since John lacks certain gospel passages such as the

11

woe against the rich and the parable of the rich man who shuns Lazarus, John has been characterized as being otherworldly and unconcerned for the poor. But if we read John through a lens focused not on "the poor" but on "the marginalized," we may begin to see what John has to say about the realities of this world. This commentary pays particular attention to the fact that Jesus and his disciples gave alms to the poor, that Jesus cured the physically afflicted, that he befriended those who were ignorant of the law, that he dealt graciously with a person marginalized because of her nationality. Nicodemus, who marginalizes people, actually becomes a disciple of Jesus and thereby joins the ranks of the marginalized. Moreover, we must notice John's great concern for marginalized women: the Samaritan woman, Martha and Mary, Mary of Magdala. Finally, the Messiah who befriended and ministered to the marginalized himself became marginalized. Condemned by both religious and political authorities, as the crucified he became the symbol of all marginalized people.

John's Situation

Most scholars date John's Gospel around 90 AD, after the Romans had destroyed Jerusalem, when that part of the Jewish community who followed and worshiped Messiah Jesus as Lord and Son of God were separating themselves from the rest. The Gospel itself provides evidence for this in the mention of "being cast out of the synagogue" in 9:22; 12:42; 16:2. John 9:22, the story of Jesus' giving sight to the man born blind, is most illustrative. The man's parents said that he was of age "because they were afraid of the Jews, for the Jews had already agreed that if anyone acknowledged Jesus as the Messiah, he would be expelled from the synagogue." John's Gospel also refers frequently to "the Jews." Given that the author of the Fourth Gospel was a Jew, this is a strange way of speaking. Scholars agree that John uses this epithet not to inspire anti-Judaism, but to designate that group of Jews who do not believe in Messiah Jesus. Considering Jesus' focus on the marginalized, however, suggests another possibility. Since ancient Judaism concerned itself not so much with orthodoxy, but with orthopraxy, perhaps "the Jews" opposed the Johannine Messianic Jews because they were admitting into their ranks marginalized people such as Samaritans and those ignorant of the Law. That is, "the Jews" were agitated not because Johannine belief bordered on ditheism, but because their practice of welcoming the marginalized was diluting the elected people of God.

Although John's is truly a Jewish Gospel, it was written while Rome held the known world in subjection. The Evangelist is not afraid to paint a picture of an ignoble Pilate. Jesus provides an abundance of drink and food just as the Roman emperors were supposed to do. Thomas professes his faith in Jesus — "My Lord and God" — in the same terms that Emperor Domitian wanted used of himself. In brief, John's Gospel being "spiritual" does not prevent it from tangling with temporal authorities who boasted that they alone had the power over life and death (see 19:10–12).

The Style of John's Gospel

John's Gospel is written with a simple vocabulary and syntax that most beginning students in New Testament Greek have no trouble reading. While John's language and sentence structure may be simple, the Gospel is replete with sophisticated literary devices that serve its theology. The Evangelist uses double-meaning words, irony, metaphor, and symbolism. For example, Jesus' use of a double-meaning word leads Nicodemus to gross misunderstanding. The Greek word *anothen* can mean "from above" or "again." When Jesus refers to being born *anothen*, Nicodemus understands him to be suggesting that a grown person must re-enter his mother's womb and be born again (see 3:3–7). John's account of Jesus' trial before Pilate is full of irony. Believers know that Jesus, robed in purple and wearing a crown of thorns and mocked as king, is really King.

John's Gospel contains many sayings in which Jesus describes himself with metaphors: "I am the noble shepherd"; "I am the bread of life"; "I am the light of the world"; "I am the vine"; "I am the resurrection and the life." Their meaning often arises from Old Testament parallels and the context of the discourses in which Jesus pronounces them. As readers become more familiar with the vocabulary and style of John's Gospel, its symbols become more evident. When Judas leaves the Last Supper, the Evangelist observes: "And it was night" (13:30) for a reason. John 21:1–14, the episode in which the Risen Jesus appears to the disciples while they are fishing on the Sea of Tiberias, is loaded with symbolism. It contains the numbers 7 and 153, signifying completeness. Then the net, although loaded with large fish, does not tear. On top of that, there is a charcoal fire, the same sort of fire that burned in the courtyard of the high priest when Peter denied Jesus thrice. The Risen Jesus provides a meal of bread and fish. The one who had provided abundant food while he was alive continues to do so after his death. John may write in simple language, but his text conveys much richness.

From time to time in John's Gospel, some things don't quite hang together. Why, in 14:31, does Jesus say: "Get up, let us go," and then continue talking for three more chapters? Why is there a chapter 21 when John 20:30–31 seems to be a conclusion? Such inconsistencies have led scholars to conclude that John's Gospel was written in stages and assembled by a final editor who belonged to the Johannine community. That may be so; nevertheless, every verse of John's Gospel is canonical.

Did the Evangelist know the Gospels of Matthew, Mark, and Luke? Surely, he didn't know them in written form. However, he seems to have known oral traditions that became part of the written texts of the Synoptics. For example, Mark 6:34–52 joins together a miracle of Jesus feeding five thousand and the miracle of him walking on water. The same two miracles are linked in John 6:1–21. John, for his part, draws hardly any attention to the miracle of Jesus walking on water, as he moves quickly to interpret the sign of Jesus multiplying bread for five thousand. It seems that John was bound by tradition to link the two miracles, although he did not choose to explore the Christological significance of Jesus walking on water.

Structure and Outline of John's Gospel

Scholars usually outline the Gospel of John by dividing it into chapters 1–12, The Book of Signs, and chapters 13–21, The Book of Glory. That is the arrangement Fr. Raymond E. Brown, S.S. used in his famous two-volume commentary in the Anchor Bible. The fluid and dynamic nature of John's Gospel, with its multiple overlapping themes, suggest to some that a new outline is in order. The one in this volume, adapted from Fernando F. Segovia's, allows greater emphasis upon the representative figures so key to John's goal of nurturing faith. In the course of his journey, Jesus encounters people on their own journeys and invites them to join him on his.

Narrative of the Word's journey to become flesh among us (1:1–18)

Narrative of the Word's public life of journeying (1:19–17:26)

First Galilee/Jerusalem Cycle (1:19–3:36)

1. John the Witness as representative figure at Bethany beyond the Jordan (1:19–34).

2. Jesus' disciples as representative figures as Jesus leaves for Galilee (1:35–51).

3. First sign in Cana of Galilee and Mother of Jesus as representative figure (2:1–12).

4. Jesus goes to Jerusalem for Passover and cleanses the temple; "the Jews" object (2:13–25).

5. In Jerusalem Jesus encounters the representative figure Nicodemus, "a ruler of the Jews" (3:1–21).

6. Jesus and John contrasted (3:22–4:2).

Second Galilee/Jerusalem Cycle (4:3–5:47)

1. Jesus passes through Samaria on his way to Galilee and encounters the representative figure of the Samaritan woman (4:3–42).

2. Jesus goes into Galilee and encounters the representative figure of the Galilean royal official (4:43–54), and for his benefit performs a second sign.

3. Jesus goes up to Jerusalem and performs a third sign upon the man who had been infirm for thirty-eight years, another representative figure (5:1–15).

4. In Jerusalem, Jesus debates with the Jews over the genuine meaning of his healing on the Sabbath (5:16–47).

Third Galilee/Jerusalem Cycle (6:1–10:42)

1. In Galilean area Jesus works a fourth sign, the multiplication of barley loaves (6:1–15).

2. Jesus performs a fifth sign, walking on Sea of Galilee (6:16–21).

3. Jesus gives his bread of life discourse in synagogue at Capernaum; "the Jews" and some disciples object (6:22–72).

4. In Jerusalem for the Feast of Tabernacles, Jesus meets opposition from "the Jews" (7:1–52).

5. Jesus and "the Jews" get into another debate over his significance (8:1–59).

6. After working his sixth sign, giving sight to the man born blind (a representative figure), Jesus is thrown out of the synagogue (9:1–41).

7. In Jerusalem Jesus teaches that he is the noble shepherd and again debates with "the Jews" over his status with his Father (10:1–39).

8. Jesus leaves Jerusalem and goes to the place where John first baptized (10:40–42).

Fourth and Final Journey to Jerusalem via Bethany (11:1–17:26)

1. Jesus goes to Bethany, very close to Jerusalem, to perform his seventh and final sign, the raising of Lazarus, brother of the representative figures Martha and Mary. Jesus' giving life to Lazarus leads to the decision that Jesus be put to death (11:1–54).

2. Jesus returns to Bethany from Ephrem. The anointing of Jesus by Mary and the criticism of her action by Judas contrast two representative figures (11:55–12:11).

3. Jesus' final entry into Jerusalem (12:12–50).

4. The context of Jesus' farewell consolation for his disciples: the foot washing (13:1–30).

5. Jesus' farewell speeches of consolation to his disciples (13:31–17:26):
   13:31–14:31: Jesus is going away, but will not leave his disciples orphans.
   15:1–16:4a: Jesus is the vine that will nourish his disciples who are persecuted.
   16:4b–33: Jesus is departing, but will give his disciples another Paraclete.
   17:1–26: Jesus' prayer of departure.

Narrative of Jesus' Death, Resurrection Appearances, and Return to the Father (18:1–21:25)

1. The ruling authorities arrest Jesus (18:1–12).

2. Jesus appears before the Jewish authorities (18:13–27).

3. Jesus appears before the Gentile authorities in the person of Pilate, a representative figure (18:28–19:16).

4. Jesus dies with words to the representative figures of his Mother and the Beloved Disciple (19:17–30).

5. The representative figure Nicodemus accompanies Joseph of Arimathea (19:31–42).

6. In Jerusalem, Jesus appears to the representative figure Mary Magdalene (20:1–2, 11–18).

7. Jesus appears to disciples and Thomas, representative figures, in Jerusalem (20:19–29).

8. The purpose of the gospel is faith (20:30–31).

9. Appearance of Jesus to his wayward disciples in Galilee (21:1–14).

10. Peter's reconciliation (21:15–25).

I

Narrative of the Word's Journey to Become Flesh Among Us (1:1–18)

John 1:1–18: A Series of Beginnings

[1] In the beginning was the Word,/ and the Word was with God, and the Word was God./ [2] He was in the beginning with God./ [3] All things came to be through him,/ and without him nothing came to be./ What came to be [4] through him was life,/ and this life was the light of the human race;/ [5] the light shines in the darkness, and the darkness has not overcome it./ [6] A man named John was sent from God. [7] He came for testimony, to testify to the light, so that all might believe through him. [8] He was not the light, but came to testify to the light. [9] The true light, which enlightens everyone, was coming into the world./ [10] He was in the world,/ and the world came to be through him,/ but the world did not know him./ [11] He came to what was his own,/ but his own people did not accept him./ [12] But to those who did accept him he gave power to become children of God, to those who believe in his name, [13] who were born not by natural generation nor by human choice nor by a man's decision but of God./ [14] And the Word became flesh/ and made his dwelling among us,/ and we saw his glory,/ the glory as of the Father's only Son,/ full of grace and truth./ [15] John testified to him and cried out, saying, "This was he of whom I said, 'The one who is coming after me ranks ahead of me because he existed before me.' " [16] From his fullness we have all received, grace in place of

grace, [17] because while the law was given through Moses, grace and truth came through Jesus Christ. [18] No one has ever seen God. The only Son, God, who is at the Father's side, has revealed him.

The Evangelist's Prologue speaks about beginnings. At the very beginning, before the world came to be, the Word was with God. John echoes Genesis 1, which opens with "In the beginning" and tells of the power of God's word to create, the power of God's light to banish darkness. This Prologue previews the Gospel's plot: The Word "came to what was his own,/ but his own people did not accept him./ But to those who did accept him he gave power to become children of God, to those who believe in his name" (1:11–12). It also foreshadows many of the themes that pulse through the Gospel: light, life, glory, world, belief, witness. Of all these beginnings, however, the most extraordinary is trumpeted in 1:14: "And the Word became flesh/ and made his dwelling among us." God is no longer speaking as before in a less complete, more limited way through the Law given to Moses on Mount Sinai, nor through prophets or psalmists, nor through Lady Wisdom, but through the human words, signs, and love of Jesus of Nazareth, his Son, whom God has sent into the world.

The allusion to Genesis 1 suggests other Old Testament passages just beneath the surface of the rest of the Prologue. Many of the Evangelist's reflections about God's Word come from the wisdom literature, such as Proverbs 8:27–30: "When [God] established the heavens I was there,/ when he marked out the vault over the face of the deep.... Then was I beside him as his craftsman,/ and I was his delight day by day,/ Playing before him all the while." Wisdom dwells in Israel, as Sirach 24:8 says: "Then the

22

Creator of all gave me his command,/ and he who formed me chose the spot for my tent,/ Saying, 'In Jacob make your dwelling,/ in Israel your inheritance.' " In times past God's Torah provided light for Israel's journey, as Psalm 119:105 suggests: "Your word is a lamp for my feet,/ a light for my path." God's kindness and fidelity came through his covenant with his chosen people. Exodus 34:6 reads: "Thus the LORD passed before [Moses] and cried out, 'The LORD, the LORD, a merciful and gracious God, slow to anger and rich in kindness and fidelity." Now God's kindness and fidelity (in John's language "grace and truth") have come through Jesus Christ. These Old Testament references help us begin to glimpse a dominant theme in the remainder of the Gospel: Jesus is the replacement of Old Testament institutions and feasts. For example, Jesus is God's dwelling, God's Temple, the light of the world.

For decades now scholars have called John's Prologue "a hymn" or "creedal hymn." This means that the Prologue is not meant merely to be read or recited. It is to be prayed. Furthermore, this hymn contains the faith that stands behind this Gospel, the faith of the Johannine community. Notice the "we" in 1:14: "And we saw his glory"; and in 1:16: "From his fullness we have all received, grace in place of grace." One way of praying the Prologue is to take our place with John the Witness (1:6–8, 15), stop the action, and view what the Prologue reveals from John's vantage point. In other words, the Prologue is not describing something external, but something that affects the interior, that wants to involve readers for dear life. Through his Gospel the Evangelist wants to deepen his readers' faith, as he shares with them his community's faith.

When I first studied John's Prologue, I was assigned to write a paper showing how the Prologue contains all the themes of the Gospel. The professor cautioned us that although the word "Word" does not recur in the rest of the Gospel, that doesn't mean that "Word" should be off our radar screen, for the many discourses of Jesus are really words of "the Word." That assignment made such an impression on me that I pursued graduate work in New Testament studies. I wanted to become an exegete like Jesus, the exegete of the Father (1:18).

II

First Galilee/Jerusalem Cycle (1:19–3:36)

John 1:19–34: John the Baptist Has
Become John the Witness

[19] And this is the testimony of John. When the Jews from Jerusalem sent priests and Levites [to him] to ask him, "Who are you?" [20] he admitted and did not deny it, but admitted, "I am not the Messiah." [21] So they asked him, "What are you then? Are you Elijah?" And he said, "I am not." "Are you the Prophet?" He answered, "No." [22] So they said to him, "Who are you, so we can give an answer to those who sent us? What do you have to say for yourself?" [23] He said:/ "I am 'the voice of one crying out in the desert,/ "Make straight the way of the Lord," '/ as Isaiah the prophet said." [24] Some Pharisees were also sent. [25] They asked him, "Why then do you baptize if you are not the Messiah or Elijah or the Prophet?" [26] John answered them, "I baptize with water; but there is one among you whom you do not recognize, [27] the one who is coming after me, whose sandal strap I am not worthy to untie." [28] This happened in Bethany across the Jordan, where John was baptizing.

[29] The next day he saw Jesus coming toward him and said, "Behold, the Lamb of God, who takes away the sin of the world. [30] He is the one of whom I said, 'A man is coming after me who ranks ahead of me because he existed before me.' [31] I did not know him, but the reason why I came baptizing with water was that he might be made known to Israel." [32] John testified further, saying,

"I saw the Spirit come down like a dove from the sky and remain upon him. [33] I did not know him, but the one who sent me to baptize with water told me, 'On whomever you see the Spirit come down and remain, he is the one who will baptize with the holy Spirit.' [34] Now I have seen and testified that he is the Son of God."

To "Let John Be John," it is necessary to distinguish his account from those of the other three evangelists. This is certainly true in the case of John the Baptist. The Fourth Gospel's first account of him, 1:19–34, does not describe what he wore and what he ate. Contrast this passage with Mark 1:6: "John was clothed in camel's hair, with a leather belt around his waist. He fed on locusts and wild honey." Luke 7:33 reads: "… John the Baptist came neither eating food nor drinking wine, and you said, 'He is possessed by a demon.' " The Fourth Gospel does not present him as an ascetic who proclaims repentance by his very way of life. Neither does it have him condemn Pharisees and Sadducees as "a brood of vipers" (Matt 3:7), nor does he tell the crowds to share their surplus clothing and food with the needy and tell the tax collectors and soldiers not to abuse their power (Luke 3:10–14). While the Fourth Gospel later notes (3:24) "John had not yet been imprisoned," it does not indicate who threw him into prison or why, information supplied by Mark: "Herod was the one who had John arrested, and bound in prison on account of Herodias, the wife of his brother Philip, whom he had married" (6:17). Perhaps the most surprising difference between the Fourth Gospel and the others is that it does describe John baptizing Jesus. It presents John not as The Baptist, but as the witness to Jesus.

26

The other three Gospels generally present trial scenes, with witnesses for and against the accused, in their later sections, as part of their passion accounts. The Fourth Gospel, however, begins its narrative of Jesus, the one sent by God, with trial scenes and witnesses and continues with subsequent trial scenes, such as the one in chapter 5. The Fourth Gospel portrays John the Baptist as one of those who witness to Jesus. "John ... came for testimony, to testify to the light.... He was not the light" (1:6–8). John 1:15 states: "John testified to him and cried out, saying, "This is he of whom I said, 'The one who is coming after me ranks ahead of me because he existed before me.' " Later (5:33) Jesus says, "You sent emissaries to John, and he testified to the truth." Finally, in 10:41 the people comment: "John performed no sign, but everything John said about this man [Jesus] was true."

The Fourth Gospel's first account of John begins with a reference to his giving testimony ("And this is the testimony of John" [1:19]), and ends with a reference to his testimony ("Now I have seen and testified that he is the Son of God" [1:34]). The Evangelist tells his readers that he is going to present John as the witness, presents him as a witness, and then concludes with a summary of John the Baptist's testimony. The Jewish leaders in Jerusalem clearly do not send an investigating team to John out of mere curiosity. They sense that something of big religious and political significance is taking place. John's testimony to them in 1:19–28 deflects attention from himself and points them in the direction of Jesus. As John 1:27 indicates, John the Baptist does not consider himself worthy to unfasten the strap of the sandal of the one to come after him.

Verses 29 to 34 present further dimensions of John's testimony. Jesus is the Lamb of God, who takes away the sins of the world (1:29). This is the closest John's Gospel will come to the foundational statement of Mark (10:45) about the significance of Jesus' death: "For the Son of Man did not come to be served but to serve and to give his life as a ransom for many." In 1:30 John bears witness to Jesus' pre-existence, a theme accentuated in the Prologue. In 1:32–33 he gives testimony to Jesus' possession and bestowal of the Holy Spirit (as in 20:22, which states "[H]e breathed on [his disciples] and said to them, 'Receive the holy Spirit …' "). His testimony concludes with the statement, "Now I have seen and testified that he is the Son of God" (1:34): Jesus is the one specially elected by God.

Contemporary novels, television shows, and movies that deal with attorneys, witnesses, juries, judges, and trials have made us familiar with the term "credible witness," one whose testimony a jury will believe. It seems that the ambassadors from Jerusalem (1:19–28) found John a credible witness, for Jesus says that the Jewish religious leaders found him to be "a burning and shining lamp, and for a while [they] were content to rejoice in his light" (5:35). Nevertheless, they stopped short of accepting John's testimony about Jesus completely. Each year the liturgy celebrates the birth of John the Baptist (Luke 1) and his martyrdom (Mark 6), but John's Gospel celebrates his role as witness and presents him as its first representative figure. Despite potential opposition to his message and role John bears steadfast witness. Are we so steadfast in similar circumstances? How comfortable are we with playing second fiddle to Jesus, of being a moon to Jesus the sun?

John 1:35–51: Disciples Recruit One Another for Jesus

[35] The next day John was there again with two of his disciples, [36] and as he watched Jesus walk by, he said, "Behold, the Lamb of God." [37] The two disciples heard what he said and followed Jesus. [38] Jesus turned and saw them following him and said to them, "What are you looking for?" They said to him, "Rabbi" (which translated means Teacher), "where are you staying?" [39] He said to them, "Come, and you will see." So they went and saw where he was staying, and they stayed with him that day. It was about four in the afternoon. [40] Andrew, the brother of Simon Peter, was one of the two who heard John and followed Jesus. [41] He first found his own brother Simon and told him, "We have found the Messiah" (which is translated Anointed). [42] Then he brought him to Jesus. Jesus looked at him and said, "You are Simon the son of John; you will be called Kephas" (which is translated Peter).

[43] The next day he decided to go to Galilee, and he found Philip. And Jesus said to him, "Follow me." [44] Now Philip was from Bethsaida, the town of Andrew and Peter. [45] Philip found Nathanael and told him, "We have found the one about whom Moses wrote in the law, and also the prophets, Jesus, son of Joseph, from Nazareth." [46] But Nathanael said to him, "Can anything good come from Nazareth?" Philip said to him, "Come and see." [47] Jesus saw Nathanael coming toward him and said of him, "Here is a true Israelite. There is no duplicity in him." [48] Nathanael said to him, "How do you know me?" Jesus answered and said to him, "Before Philip called you, I saw you under the fig tree." [49] Nathanael answered him, "Rabbi, you are the Son of God; you are the King of Israel." [50] Jesus answered and said to him, "Do you believe because I told you that I

saw you under the fig tree? You will see greater things than this." [51] And he said to him, "Amen, amen, I say to you, you will see the sky opened and the angels of God ascending and descending on the Son of Man."

In 1:35–51 Jesus does not call fishermen. Only in 21:1–14 do we learn that some of the disciples were fishermen. In this passage Jesus does not give Peter a prominent role as he does in Luke 5:10, when he says, "from now on you will be catching men." Peter, Andrew, James, and John do not leave their boats, nets, and family to follow Jesus as Mark describes them doing (1:16–20). Rather Andrew and his companion abandon John the Baptist and his way of life to follow Jesus, and then Andrew goes in pursuit of his brother, Peter.

Three other points are important here. Father Raymond E. Brown is surely correct in saying that profound questions about the very meaning of life lie hidden deep inside the two questions of 1:38: "Jesus turned and saw them following him and said to them, 'What are you looking for?' They said to him, 'Rabbi' (which translated means Teacher), 'where are you staying?'" Jesus answers both questions in the next verse: "Come, and you will see." It's an invitation to every follower of Jesus, and that is why John's Gospel, as the outline in my Introduction indicates, is a journey of discovery.

The representative figure of this passage is a little-known figure to whom the Evangelist devotes six whole verses — Nathanael, from Cana in Galilee (21:2). Commentators puzzle over the reference to the fig tree under which Jesus saw him. Perhaps it is an allusion to rabbis studying the meaning of Scripture, as one would search deeper and deeper into the recesses of a tree to find more

30

fruit. In any case it seems clear that Nathanael is an example of a person who knows Moses and the prophets, believes that someone from Nazareth cannot fulfill the Law and the prophets, yet changes his mind when he comes into the presence of Jesus, who has superior knowledge. Nathanael confesses: "[Y]ou are the Son of God; you are the King of Israel" (1:49). Yet what he sees now pales in comparison to what God will reveal in Jesus throughout the rest of the Gospel (1:51). Nathanael truly sees because there is no duplicity in him, unlike many others, such as the parade of individuals in John 9 who have superior knowledge of the Scriptures, yet despite Jesus' actions still refuse to change their minds.

In this passage Jesus has said little and certainly has performed no sign, yet his first disciples exalt him with lofty titles of faith: Messiah (1:41); the one spoken about in the Law and the prophets (1:45); the Son of God, the King of Israel (1:49). This Gospel describes the disciples journeying with Jesus back and forth from Galilee to Jerusalem, listening to his discourses and witnessing his signs. Their faith and that of contemporary readers will deepen, especially when they realize that when that Son of Man upon whom angels ascend and descend is lifted up on the cross, God is revealed. As Jesus says in 8:28: "When you lift up the Son of Man, then you will realize that I AM," that is, that Jesus is God.

A careful reading of John 1 reveals the wonderful difference between this Gospel and those of Matthew, Mark, and Luke. When we let John be John, we can appreciate, be challenged by, and be strengthened by his presentation of Jesus.

John 2:1–11: Jesus Gives Life Abundantly

¹ On the third day there was a wedding in Cana in Galilee, and the mother of Jesus was there. ² Jesus and his disciples were also invited to the wedding. ³ When the wine ran short, the mother of Jesus said to him, "They have no wine." ⁴ [And] Jesus said to her, "Woman, how does your concern affect me? My hour has not yet come." ⁵ His mother said to the servers, "Do whatever he tells you." ⁶ Now there were six stone water jars there for Jewish ceremonial washings, each holding twenty to thirty gallons. ⁷ Jesus told them, "Fill the jars with water." So they filled them to the brim. ⁸ Then he told them, "Draw some out now and take it to the headwaiter." So they took it. ⁹ And when the headwaiter tasted the water that had become wine, without knowing where it came from (although the servers who had drawn the water knew), the headwaiter called the bridegroom ¹⁰ and said to him, "Everyone serves good wine first, and then when people have drunk freely, an inferior one; but you have kept the good wine until now." ¹¹ Jesus did this as the beginning of his signs in Cana in Galilee and so revealed his glory, and his disciples began to believe in him.

Only John's Gospel narrates this striking miracle, Jesus' first sign (2:11). It is first because it contains the foundation for the remaining signs, setting the pattern for those that follow.

Scholars speak of the "realized eschatology" of the Fourth Gospel; that is, in Jesus' ministry what is expected to come only at the end of time, at the *eschaton* (a Greek word that means "last things"), is already being realized. Amos 9:13–14 speaks about the last days: "Yes, days are coming,/ says the LORD,/ when the plowman shall overtake the reaper..../ The juice of grapes shall drip down the mountains,/ and all the hills shall run with it..../ [T]hey shall .../ Plant vineyards and drink the wine.... " Isaiah 25:6–8 also uses wine imagery to describe the eschaton: "On this mountain the LORD of hosts/ will provide for all peoples/ A feast of rich food and choice wines,/ juicy, rich food and pure, choice wines...." A second-century AD Jewish pseudepigraphical text, 2 Baruch, presents this lip-smacking prediction: "The earth will also yield fruits ten thousandfold. And on one vine will be a thousand branches, and one branch will produce a thousand clusters, and one cluster will produce a thousand grapes, and one grape will produce 300 liters of wine" (29:5, translation by A. F. J. Klijn). Jesus' first sign at Cana provides the bridegroom and his guests enough of the finest wine to satisfy any oenophile — 600 liters, or 50 cases. In a tiny village where people would ordinarily drink one liter of diluted wine a day, this new supply would last a week and make everybody overjoyed. Jesus' wine supplants the water of Jewish purification and thereby announces a theme that will occupy the Evangelist's attention time and again in the rest of his narrative. Furthermore, Jesus appears as a new ruler and Lord, for Roman emperors likened themselves to the god Dionysius who supplied abundantly flowing wine. The Evangelist is saying: Step aside, Caesar, for a new giver of life-supplying wine is here — Jesus.

Jesus' signs also give narrative expression to Jesus' hour and glory, because what Jesus' death on the cross and glorification accomplish are anticipated in his signs. Or as John 2:11 says: Jesus "so revealed his glory, and his disciples began to believe in him." Thus, Jesus cures a child ravaged by fever (4:46–54), heals a man incapacitated for thirty-eight years (5:1–15), feeds five thousand with abundant food (6:1–15), gives sight to a man born blind (9:1–41), resuscitates a man (Lazarus) who had been dead for four days (11:1–44), and lays down his life and takes it up again (chapters 19–20).

Over the centuries commentators have puzzled over Jesus' treatment of his Mother. Three comments may shed some light on John 2:3–4. In John's narrative world Jesus will not be forced by anyone, even someone as close to him as his Mother, to do anything. Thus Jesus demurs when the royal official requests that Jesus come to cure the official's son. In 7:1–10 Jesus' relatives cannot force him to go to the feast. Jesus will go when he wants to. Despite the entreaties of his dearest friends, Martha and Mary, Jesus bides his time and then finally goes to see Lazarus (11:4–6). Second, when Jesus' Mother next appears in John's Gospel, at the foot of the cross, he entrusts her to the care of the Beloved Disciple (19:25–27). Her reappearance in a most positive light at that most significant moment in the Gospel points to her as a representative figure of those who wait patiently for salvation and blessings from Jesus. This last point leads into a third observation that highlights Jesus' Mother's words in 2:5: "Do whatever he tells you." This is a command based on trust and faith in the salvific power of her son.

Episodes such as the miracle at the wedding feast of Cana suggest that John's Gospel works on two levels — the literal and the figurative. Wine is for drinking, but its abundance also signifies God's blessings at the end of time. As St. Bonaventure observed some 750 years ago, this story tells us that Jesus was not against marriage and the enjoyment of alcoholic beverages. Moreover, it shows that Word became flesh for human joy and celebration, symbolized so powerfully and wondrously in premium wine by the case.

John 2:12–22: Jesus Replaces Jewish Worship

[12] After this, he and his mother, [his] brothers, and his disciples went down to Capernaum and stayed there only a few days.
[13] Since the Passover of the Jews was near, Jesus went up to Jerusalem. [14] He found in the temple area those who sold oxen, sheep, and doves, as well as the money-changers seated there. [15] He made a whip out of cords and drove them all out of the temple area, with the sheep and oxen, and spilled the coins of the money-changers and overturned their tables, [16] and to those who sold doves he said, "Take these out of here, and stop making my Father's house a marketplace." [17] His disciples recalled the words of scripture, "Zeal for your house will consume me." [18] At this the Jews answered and said to him, "What sign can you show us for doing this?" [19] Jesus answered and said to them, "Destroy this temple and in three days I will raise it up." [20] The Jews said, "This temple has been under construction for forty-six years, and you will raise it up in three days?" [21] But he was speaking about the temple of his body. [22] Therefore, when he was raised from the dead, his disciples remembered that he had said this, and they came to believe the scripture and the word Jesus had spoken.

Once liberated from the constraints of their accustomed ways of hearing scripture only in snippets or the tendency to homogenize all of the evangelists' different versions of the gospel, readers may truly see the uniqueness of this and other passages from John. His version of the so-called cleansing of the Temple occurs at the beginning of Jesus' ministry, not at its end as the Synoptics place it in their narratives (Matthew 21:12–13; Mark 11:15–17; Luke 19:45–46). Readers who recognize this passage only from the lectionary or who harmonize it with the versions of Matthew, Mark, and Luke will miss its weighty significance. They need to let John be John!

Not only has Jesus come for the first time to Jerusalem, but he has done so for the Feast of Passover, the celebration of God delivering the chosen people from slavery. The first sign at Cana only alluded to Jesus' supplanting one particular Jewish ritual, purification (2:6), with the superabundance that he has brought to the world; this passage, however, gives clear and unequivocal expression to his reconstituting Jewish worship, a theme that John sounds again and again, as in 5:1 ("a certain feast"), 6:4 (Passover), 7:2 (Tabernacles), 10:22 (Dedication). Key to John's account in 2:13–17 are the Scripture citations in 2:16–17. Zechariah 14:21, quoted by Jesus in 2:16, refers to the day of God's eschatological restoration of Jerusalem and its Temple: "On that day there shall no longer be any merchant in the house of the Lord of hosts." Psalm 69:9–10, quoted in 2:17, reads: "I have become an outcast to my kin..../ Because zeal for your house consumes me,/ I am scorned by those who scorn you."

Only after Jesus' resurrection and under the inspiration of the Paraclete who leads disciples into the truth of what Jesus said and did (14:26) do the disciples (and we too, today) understand how Psalm 69 applies to Jesus' action

36

in the Temple. If the animals of sacrifice no longer exist in the Temple and if the special imageless coins needed to pay for animals and the maintenance of the Temple have been tossed out, then in a prophetic action Jesus has stopped the worship of former times.

John 2:18–22 announces a theme that recurs in this Gospel: confrontation between Jesus and the Jewish elite over what he says or does. They fail to see the significance of Jesus' prophetic sign of driving out their means of worship and demand that he perform a stupendous miracle to justify his actions. Lacking the insight of believers who read this Gospel, they misunderstand Jesus' answer because they take it literally: "Destroy this temple and in three days I will raise it up." Truly, Jesus "was speaking about the temple of his body" (2:21) where worship will now take place. John 2:22 offers consolation for those who still may misunderstand Jesus' words: "Therefore, when he was raised from the dead, his disciples remembered that he had said this, and they came to believe the scripture and the word Jesus had spoken."

Reading John's "different" Gospel is no easy task, for he may use events that readers may already recognize from the Gospels of Mark, Matthew, and Luke, but through diction or placement he gives them a different twist. Readers have to know Scripture and be willing to be jolted out of a literal way of reading that may lead to misunderstanding. Jesus, the one sent from the Father, is zealous to reveal God, to show that he is God's presence among men and women. This zeal that consumes him will cause many, even the Jewish elite, to reject him, and will lead to his death.

John 2:23–25: Signs Aplenty, but Where Is Deep Faith?

23 While he was in Jerusalem for the feast of Passover, many began to believe in his name when they saw the signs he was doing. 24 But Jesus would not trust himself to them because he knew them all, 25 and did not need anyone to testify about human nature. He himself understood it well.

Although the Evangelist narrates only Jesus' prophetic "cleansing of the Temple," Jesus seems to have performed a number of signs in Jerusalem during the Feast of Passover. See also John 4:45 where this is said of the Galileans: "They had seen all he had done in Jerusalem at the feast; for they themselves had gone to the feast." Even though these people may have seen Jesus' signs, their sight did not lead them to believe that he was the one sent by the Father. See John 6:26 where Jesus says to those who have enjoyed the results of his sign of the multiplication of loaves: "Jesus answered them and said, 'Amen, amen, I say to you, you are looking for me not because you saw signs but because you ate the loaves and were filled.' " These individuals seek Jesus because of their bellies, not because of their faith. The Evangelist concludes chapter 2 with a reference to Jesus' divine gift of understanding what lies within men and women: He "did not need anyone to testify about human nature. He himself understood it well." Jesus has come not to feed and entertain people but to reveal to them the Father. The "many [who] began to believe in his name when they saw the signs he was doing" represent those whose vision is faulty, those content with surface meanings, unable or unwilling to make the jump to a deeper understanding.

John 3:1–21: Nicodemus Begins to See the Light;
Jesus, Lifted Up On the Cross, Saves

[1] Now there was a Pharisee named Nicodemus, a ruler of the Jews. [2] He came to Jesus at night and said to him, "Rabbi, we know that you are a teacher who has come from God, for no one can do these signs that you are doing unless God is with him." [3] Jesus answered and said to him, "Amen, amen, I say to you, no one can see the kingdom of God without being born from above." [4] Nicodemus said to him, "How can a person once grown old be born again? Surely he cannot reenter his mother's womb and be born again, can he?" [5] Jesus answered, "Amen, amen, I say to you, no one can enter the kingdom of God without being born of water and Spirit. [6] What is born of flesh is flesh and what is born of spirit is spirit. [7] Do not be amazed that I told you, 'You must be born from above.' [8] The wind blows where it wills, and you can hear the sound it makes, but you do not know where it comes from or where it goes; so it is with everyone who is born of the Spirit." [9] Nicodemus answered and said to him, "How can this happen?" [10] Jesus answered and said to him, "You are the teacher of Israel and you do not understand this? [11] Amen, amen, I say to you, we speak of what we know and we testify to what we have seen, but you people do not accept our testimony. [12] If I tell you about earthly things and you do not believe, how will you believe if I tell you about heavenly things? [13] No one has gone up to heaven except the one who has come down from heaven, the Son of Man. [14] And just as Moses lifted up the serpent in the desert, so must the Son of Man be lifted up, [15] so that everyone who believes in him may have eternal life."

[16] For God so loved the world that he gave his only Son, so that everyone who believes in him might not perish but might have eternal life. [17] For God did not send his Son into the world to condemn the world, but that the world might be saved through him. [18] Whoever

believes in him will not be condemned, but whoever does not believe has already been condemned, because he has not believed in the name of the only Son of God. [19] And this is the verdict, that the light came into the world, but people preferred darkness to light, because their works were evil. [20] For everyone who does wicked things hates the light and does not come toward the light, so that his works might not be exposed. [21] But whoever lives the truth comes to the light, so that his works may be clearly seen as done in God.

This passage, which presents another representative figure, Nicodemus, can be divided into two sections: 3:1–10 and 3:11–21. Some scholars who examine this passage, especially 3:1–10, consider Nicodemus a negative representative figure because he comes "at night" (3:2) and seems to belong to those who "preferred darkness to light" (3:20). His faith is on the level of signs; that is, he is taken up with Jesus' wonders and doesn't consider that the person who works these signs may be the one sent by God. Moreover, he seems to misunderstand Jesus' teaching and so deserves to be put in his place: "Jesus answered and said to him, 'You are the teacher of Israel and you do not understand this?' " (3:10).

In Nicodemus' favor is the fact that, although he comes to Jesus at night when no one could easily see him, he does come. He does have initial faith that can blossom into something deeper. Most importantly, John brings him back into his narrative twice more. In 7:50–52 Nicodemus defends Jesus against the judgments of the other Jewish leaders: "Does our law condemn a person before it first hears him and finds out what he is doing?" (7:51). And at the end of the Gospel, in a passage unique to John, Nicodemus joins Joseph of Arimathea to give Jesus a royal burial (19:38–42). Far from being a negative representative figure, such evidence seems to depict Nicodemus as someone who grows in faith and his relationship with Jesus as the one sent by the Father. This is the conclusion to which St. Bonaventure, the great Franciscan exegete, arrived some 750 years ago.

Through Nicodemus' two misunderstandings John teaches his readers the benefits that Jesus brings. Nicodemus takes the Greek word *anothen* in a literal sense to mean "again," whereas Jesus intends another of its meanings, "from above." John 3:3–5 echoes 1:12–13 of the Prologue: "But to those who did accept him [the Word] he gave power to become children of God, to those who believe in his name, who were born not by natural generation nor by human choice nor by a man's decision but of God." To these concepts from the Prologue, the passage at 3:3–5 adds the words "water" and "Spirit." A person enters God's kingdom by the new birth of water and the gift of the Spirit. In 3:6–8 John continues Jesus' reflection on the role of the Spirit, leading to Nicodemus' second misunderstanding. "The flesh," that is, human beings left to their own devices and in their own frailty, cannot beget the Spirit, who comes from above, from God. Indeed, how can this happen? (3:10). John 3:11–21 presents an extended answer that shifts the focus of the passage from Nicodemus to the salvific role of Jesus.

In 3:11–21 John indicates clearly that he intends not to primarily chronicle in detail Jesus' words and deeds nor to present Jesus' personal life. A careful examination of 3:11 reveals that the "we" of which Jesus speaks is not the majestic "we," but the "we" of the believing community that the Evangelist used in 1:14: "[A]nd we saw his glory." John 3:11

reads: "[W]e speak of what we know and we testify to what we have seen, but you people do not accept our testimony." Having been begotten by God through Jesus' word in faith, members of the Johannine community know heavenly things and bear witness to them. People who do not believe or who, like Nicodemus, are at the very first beginnings of faith, do not know.

John 3:13–16 trumpets the faith of the Johannine community. Jesus is the Son of Man who is the mediator between heaven and earth. The Evangelist makes his next Christological statement by invoking Numbers 21:9: "Moses ... made a bronze serpent and mounted it on a pole and whenever anyone who had been bitten by a serpent looked at the bronze serpent that person recovered" (author's translation). Further, as he did in 3:3–4 with the Greek word *anothen* ("from above" or "again"), the Evangelist plays on two meanings of "lifted up": lifted up on a pole or lifted up on a cross. Through Jesus' death on the cross all who believe will have eternal life in him. The Evangelist will repeat this "lifting up" language in 8:28 and 12:32–34, and it may be his equivalent of Jesus' threefold prediction of his passion in the Synoptics.

At sporting events in the United States, Christians who want to share their faith in Jesus sometimes hold up for the crowd and the television cameras banners that read "John 3:16: For God so loved the world that he gave his only Son, so that everyone who believes in him might not perish but might have eternal life." This astonishing confession of faith proclaims that although the world may be hostile to God and God's purposes, God still loves it. God loves this hostile world so much that he revealed his only Son to it in human form and invites all to faith in Jesus, sent from the Father and lifted high on a cross to grant eternal life to all who believe.

John 3:17–21 concludes Jesus' discourse. Various catechisms list the four last things as: death, judgment, heaven, and hell. In John's realized eschatology the judgment expected at the end is now present in Jesus' life and ministry. Although Jesus has come for salvific judgment, there are those who do not believe in him and invite the judgment of condemnation. The Fourth Evangelist explains their lack of faith: their deeds of darkness prevent them from seeing the light. They don't want their works to be exposed as wrong. This passage echoes 1:5, "The light shines on in the darkness, a darkness that did not comprehend it" (author's translation).

Nicodemus, along with the contemporary readers whom he may represent, is listening to John 3:11–21 from the edge of the stage. The powerful proclamations of the faith of the Johannine community urge them to come to the center of the stage and join their voices to the "we" that confesses that God's power to save is mediated through his only begotten Son, lifted high on the cross.

John 3:22–36: Jesus Must Increase While John Must Decrease

22 After this, Jesus and his disciples went into the region of Judea, where he spent some time with them baptizing. 23 John was also baptizing in Aenon near Salim, because there was an abundance of water there, and people came to be baptized, 24 for John had not yet been imprisoned. 25 Now a dispute arose between the disciples of John and a Jew about ceremonial washings. 26 So they came to John and said to him, "Rabbi, the one who was with you across

the Jordan, to whom you testified, here he is baptizing and everyone is coming to him." [27] John answered and said, "No one can receive anything except what has been given him from heaven. [28] You yourselves can testify that I said [that] I am not the Messiah, but that I was sent before him. [29] The one who has the bride is the bridegroom; the best man, who stands and listens for him, rejoices greatly at the bridegroom's voice. So this joy of mine has been made complete. [30] He must increase; I must decrease."

[31] The one who comes from above is above all. The one who is of the earth is earthly and speaks of earthly things. But the one who comes from heaven [is above all]. [32] He testifies to what he has seen and heard, but no one accepts his testimony. [33] Whoever does accept his testimony certifies that God is trustworthy. [34] For the one whom God sent speaks the words of God. He does not ration his gift of the Spirit. [35] The Father loves the Son and has given everything over to him. [36] Whoever believes in the Son has eternal life, but whoever disobeys the Son will not see life, but the wrath of God remains upon him.

Jesus and his disciples continue to journey. John 3:22–30 has some parallels in the Synoptics, which compare Jesus and John the Baptist. See, for example, Luke 7:18–35. John's Gospel is unique, however, in that John does not baptize Jesus and Jesus himself does baptize. There seems to be a kernel of historical truth in the Fourth Evangelist's presentation of facts. In any case, John the Witness does not waver from the earlier testimony described in 1:19–36. Two of John's disciples had become Jesus' first followers (1:35–37); nevertheless, John rejoices in Jesus' successful ministry of baptizing and, using Old Testament imagery, explains his reaction to his remaining disciples. Isaiah 62:5

describes God's relationship to Israel as that of a bridegroom to a bride: "as a bridegroom rejoices in his bride/ so shall your God rejoice in you." John the Witness is merely the best man, not the bridegroom. In words over which many a preacher has waxed eloquently, John states: "[Jesus] must increase; I must decrease" (3:30). Except for cameo appearances in 5:33–35 and 10:40–42, John the Witness leaves the Johannine stage.

John 3:31–36 raises puzzling questions. Who is speaking — John the Witness, Jesus, or the Evangelist? If they are the words of Jesus or the Evangelist, wouldn't they fit better after 3:21, whose themes they echo? Here the untidiness of the Fourth Gospel begins to emerge. While John's entire Gospel is canonical, in its very early history it may have stemmed from several different hands. I prefer to interpret the Gospel as we have it rather than to rearrange its passages to fit purportedly more appropriate contexts. For an extreme example of recreating John's Gospel according to its various stages of editing interested readers may consult Rudolf Bultmann's outstanding and influential commentary. I believe that 3:31–36 stems from the Evangelist and deepens the theme of witness that permeates 3:26–30. The most important verses, 3:33–34, introduce two other elements in the Gospel's theme of Jesus as witness. To refuse Jesus' testimony implies that God who has sent Jesus to give witness is untruthful, not to be trusted. Put positively, "Whoever does accept his testimony certifies that God is trustworthy" (3:33). Jesus the witness has the gift of the Spirit in abundance; he does dole out the Spirit in meager installments (3:34).

In Luke 7:18–24 John the Baptist puzzles over Jesus' teaching and actions and sends two of his disciples to ask:

"When the men came to him, they said, 'John the Baptist has sent us to you to ask, "Are you the one who is to come, or should we look for another?"'" (7:20). In John's Gospel it is clear to John the Witness who Jesus is: "The one who comes from above ... and testifies to what he has seen and heard" (3:31–32). John is the best man, who, having prepared all things for the bridegroom, discreetly leaves the wedding scene: "He must increase; I must decrease" (3:30).

III

Second Galilee/Jerusalem Cycle (4:3–5:47)

4:1–42: A Non-Jewish Woman Believes and Becomes a Missionary to Fellow Outcasts

¹ Now when Jesus learned that the Pharisees had heard that Jesus was making and baptizing more disciples than John ² (although Jesus himself was not baptizing, just his disciples), ³ he left Judea and returned to Galilee.

⁴ He had to pass through Samaria. ⁵ So he came to a town of Samaria called Sychar, near the plot of land that Jacob had given to his son Joseph. ⁶ Jacob's well was there. Jesus, tired from his journey, sat down there at the well. It was about noon.

⁷ A woman of Samaria came to draw water. Jesus said to her, "Give me a drink." ⁸ His disciples had gone into the town to buy food. ⁹ The Samaritan woman said to him, "How can you, a Jew, ask me, a Samaritan woman, for a drink?" (For Jews use nothing in common with Samaritans.) ¹⁰ Jesus answered and said to her, "If you knew the gift of God and who is saying to you, 'Give me a drink,' you would have asked him and he would have given you living water." ¹¹ [The woman] said to him, "Sir, you do not even have a bucket and the cistern is deep; where then can you get this living water? ¹² Are you greater than our father Jacob, who gave us this cistern and drank from it himself with his children and his flocks?" ¹³ Jesus answered and said to her, "Everyone who drinks this water will be thirsty again; ¹⁴ but whoever drinks the water I shall give will never thirst; the

water I shall give will become in him a spring of water welling up to eternal life." ¹⁵ The woman said to him, "Sir, give me this water, so that I may not be thirsty or have to keep coming here to draw water."

¹⁶ Jesus said to her, "Go call your husband and come back." ¹⁷ The woman answered and said to him, "I do not have a husband." Jesus answered her, "You are right in saying, 'I do not have a husband.' ¹⁸ For you have had five husbands, and the one you have now is not your husband. What you have said is true." ¹⁹ The woman said to him, "Sir, I can see that you are a prophet. ²⁰ Our ancestors worshiped on this mountain; but you people say that the place to worship is in Jerusalem." ²¹ Jesus said to her, "Believe me, woman, the hour is coming when you will worship the Father neither on this mountain nor in Jerusalem. ²² You people worship what you do not understand; we worship what we understand, because salvation is from the Jews. ²³ But the hour is coming, and is now here, when true worshipers will worship the Father in Spirit and truth; and indeed the Father seeks such people to worship him. ²⁴ God is Spirit, and those who worship him must worship in Spirit and truth." ²⁵ The woman said to him, "I know that the Messiah is coming, the one called the Anointed; when he comes, he will tell us everything." ²⁶ Jesus said to her, "I am he, the one who is speaking with you."

²⁷ At that moment his disciples returned, and were amazed that he was talking with a woman, but still no one said, "What are you looking for?" or "Why are you talking with her?" ²⁸ The woman left her water jar and went into the town and said to the people, ²⁹ "Come see a man who told me everything I have done. Could he possibly be the Messiah?" ³⁰ They went out of the town and came to him. ³¹ Meanwhile, the disciples urged him, "Rabbi, eat." ³² But he said to them, "I have food to eat

of which you do not know." [33] So the disciples said to one another, "Could someone have brought him something to eat?" [34] Jesus said to them, "My food is to do the will of the one who sent me and to finish his work. [35] Do you not say, 'In four months the harvest will be here'? I tell you, look up and see the fields ripe for the harvest. [36] The reaper is already receiving his payment and gathering crops for eternal life, so that the sower and reaper can rejoice together. [37] For here the saying is verified that 'One sows and another reaps.' [38] I sent you to reap what you have not worked for; others have done the work, and you are sharing the fruits of their work."

[39] Many of the Samaritans of that town began to believe in him because of the word of the woman who testified, "He told me everything I have done." [40] When the Samaritans came to him, they invited him to stay with them; and he stayed there two days. [41] Many more began to believe in him because of his word, [42] and they said to the woman, "We no longer believe because of your word; for we have heard for ourselves, and we know that this is truly the savior of the world."

This section contains four sections: Introduction (1–6), Jesus and the Samaritan woman (7–30), Jesus and his disciples (31–38), Jesus and the Samaritans (39–42). The Introduction functions to get Jesus on the road again, from Judea to Galilee, and away from potential trouble with the Jewish religious leaders. But the interjection of verse 2 reveals a redactor's hand: "Although Jesus himself was not baptizing, just his disciples." Recall that 3:22, 26 said that Jesus was baptizing. John 4:2 may be a redactor's clumsy attempt to suggest that Jesus not baptizing as John did indicates that he occupied a position above the Baptist's.

Many are fond of John's story of Jesus and the Samaritan woman. But familiarity with this story of an outcast woman coming to belief in Jesus may conceal its true depth and complex structure. Understanding the background of this story helps to explain the apparent leaps in logic that punctuate Jesus' discussion with the Samaritan woman, such as the sudden shift after Jesus reveals her marital status to a question of worship (18–19).

First of all, to put it mildly, Jews and Samaritans did not get along ("For Jews use nothing in common with Samaritans"). As a matter of fact, in 8:48 the Jewish leaders deride Jesus as "a Samaritan." Why would Jesus want to drink from a cup polluted from contact with a half-Jew?

Second, Jesus is alone with a woman in a public place at high noon. Women came as a group to draw water in the morning and evening. Most likely, the woman is alone at the well at noon because the other Samaritan women shunned her.

Third, a motif that John often uses, misunderstanding, runs through the dialogue between the woman and Jesus over the meaning of water.

Fourth, the Samaritans worshiped on Mount Gerizim, not Mount Zion in Jerusalem. They held as sacred only the first five books of the Old Testament and expected a Messiah figure. The Jews scorned the Samaritans because they were said to worship five gods.

Fifth, the narrative reflects the Old Testament pattern of a betrothal at a well. See, for example, Genesis 24:1–67 and its lengthy tale of how Abraham secures a bride for his son Isaac. It is near evening "at the time when women go out to draw water" (24:11). Abraham's servant asks Rebekah: "Please give me a sip of water from your jug"

(24:17). Rebekah leads Abraham's servant to her family, and through Rebekah's brother, Laban, the betrothal of Rebekah to Isaac is arranged.

Finally, the narrative reflects the Old Testament motif of God as the bridegroom seeking his spouse or covenant partner, that is, God's people. See, for instance, Isaiah 62:5: "as a bridegroom rejoices in his bride/ so shall your God rejoice in you." All of these points are important to understanding this story.

The Evangelist has the disciples go into town to buy food, so that Jesus and the Samaritan woman can be alone. The disciples will return to the stage in 4:27, 31–38. Why has the Evangelist put Jesus and an outcast woman together by themselves in a public place at noon? Because Jesus is being presented as the bridegroom seeking a spouse at a well. It makes no difference that the woman Jesus woos may be a sinner with a checkered past of adultery or idolatry. As the story makes clear, this woman comes to a certain faith in Jesus. She wants the living water that quenches thirst forever and that Jesus alone can provide (10–15).

In verses 16–18 the Evangelist takes the betrothal imagery further, as Jesus sees into the woman's background and asks whether she is free to enter into a relationship of true worship through the one who gives living water. She not only acknowledges that Jesus is a prophet, but also realizes that he is not speaking about her marital status on a literal level. Rather Jesus is talking about a covenant relationship with God under the image of marriage. He uses her question about the place of worship as the entry point into a discourse about the true worship of God, awaited at the end of time, that is taking place at this very moment

(4:21–24). The woman asks Jesus who is going to bring this true worship about, and suggests what she as a Samaritan believes: "the Messiah." The full significance of Jesus' reply, "I AM" (26) emerges only against the background of Old Testament passages such as Exodus 3:14: "God replied [to Moses], 'I am who am.' Then he added, 'This is what you shall tell the Israelites: I AM sent me to you.'"

We don't really know whether the Samaritan woman caught the full meaning of Jesus' revelation of himself as "I AM," because she leaves her ordinary job of drawing water and dashes back into town. This extraordinary woman doesn't share her news only with other women, but with the entire town. Still, she doesn't reveal all that she believes about Jesus, only what she knows will interest her fellow townspeople: Jesus is one who knows what people have done in the past, and may be the Messiah that the Samaritans are expecting (4:29).

In verse 27, John reminds readers of the strangeness of Jesus talking with a woman: Not one of his disciples asked, "Why are you talking with her?" Jesus describes himself as the source of life-giving water in verses 7–15; and in 31–34 he proclaims what his food is: to do the will of the one who sent him and to bring his work to completion. Again the narrative of the Fourth Gospel works with different meanings of simple words. In this instance it is the word "food." In verses 35–38 the Evangelist introduces a reflection from the missionary activity of the Johannine community. Jesus is the sower while his disciples are those who harvest. In this context it seems that there are two sowers, Jesus and the Samaritan woman who will lead her fellow townspeople to the harvest or enjoyment of the gift she has found in Jesus. She is bringing real food to Jesus whereas the disciples carry perishable food to him to satisfy his bodily needs. At the conclusion of this remarkable story (39–42) the Samaritan woman leads her townspeople to Jesus, then backs off the scene. Like her they have been led away from inferior worship to worship of the one who "is truly the savior of the world" (42). Although "salvation is from the Jews" (22), it is not limited to them. This narrative makes it abundantly clear that under the symbol of water Jesus brings salvation to the outcast Samaritans, who gladly receive it.

The Samaritan woman is an astounding representative figure: a pariah, a sinner, an outcast who does not shy away from Jesus in his dialogue with her and ends up calling him a prophet. In response, Jesus reveals to her his divine status. In a real sense this is a love story of God in Jesus wooing sinners into a relationship comparable to the deep relationship of marriage.

John 4:43–54: A Royal Official Believes in the Word of the Word

43 After the two days, he left there for Galilee. 44 For Jesus himself testified that a prophet has no honor in his native place. 45 When he came into Galilee, the Galileans welcomed him, since they had seen all he had done in Jerusalem at the feast; for they themselves had gone to the feast.
46 Then he returned to Cana in Galilee, where he had made the water wine. Now there was a royal official whose son was ill in Capernaum. 47 When he heard that Jesus had arrived in Galilee from Judea, he went to him and asked him to come down and heal his son, who was near death. 48 Jesus said to him, "Unless you people see signs and wonders, you will not believe." 49 The royal

official said to him, "Sir, come down before my child dies." [50] Jesus said to him, "You may go; your son will live." The man believed what Jesus said to him and left. [51] While he was on his way back, his slaves met him and told him that his boy would live. [52] He asked them when he began to recover. They told him, "The fever left him yesterday, about one in the afternoon." [53] The father realized that just at that time Jesus had said to him, "Your son will live," and he and his whole household came to believe. [54] [Now] this was the second sign Jesus did when he came to Galilee from Judea.

For many, Jesus' miracle at the wedding Feast of Cana is one of their favorite gospel passages. But they overlook the fact that Jesus actually performed two signs in Cana. In both, Jesus worked the sign by his mere word. In any case, in the person of the royal official we are dealing with yet another representative figure. Because he was a Gentile or a Galilean, the Jewish elite considered him an outcast. Galileans were considered rustics who did not observe the law with the same rigor as did the urbane residents of Jerusalem. Gentiles, of course, were not even part of the chosen people. Jesus, again on the road, realizes that both in Judea and in Galilee people marvel at the wonders of his signs but do not appreciate them as pointers to who he is. As with the first sign at Cana, there is the pattern of petition, rebuff, and then response. Jesus will act only when he wants to.

The plight of the royal official becomes more poignant in light of the historical reality in Jesus' day that half of all children died before their tenth birthday. The father, who was becoming more attached to his son, knows that he is about to lose him. The key verse in his encounter with Jesus is: "The man believed what Jesus said to him and left" (50). John's Prologue has made it clear that Jesus is the Word. Now an outcast trusts in the word of the Word, who has power over death. The magnitude of Jesus' power is also seen in the fact that he restores the boy to life by his word from a distance of some twenty-three miles.

John 2:1 to 4:54 presents a parade of representative figures. Jesus' Mother trusts in her Son. John the Baptist confesses that Jesus is above him. A Samaritan woman, a half-Jew, comes to faith in Jesus. A Gentile or Galilean royal official obediently obeys the word of the Word. How can we draw strength in our journeys of faith from these representative people?

John 5:1–15: Jesus Cures a Man of a Longstanding Illness

[1] After this, there was a feast of the Jews, and Jesus went up to Jerusalem. [2] Now there is in Jerusalem at the Sheep [Gate] a pool called in Hebrew Bethesda, with five porticoes. [3] In these lay a large number of ill, blind, lame, and crippled. [4] [5]One man was there who had been ill for thirty-eight years. [6] When Jesus saw him lying there and knew that he had been ill for a long time, he said to him, "Do you want to be well?" [7] The sick man answered him, "Sir, I have no one to put me into the pool when the water is stirred up; while I am on my way, someone else gets down there before me." [8] Jesus said to him, "Rise, take up your mat, and walk." [9] Immediately the man became well, took up his mat, and walked.

Now that day was a sabbath. [10] So the Jews said to the man who was cured, "It is the sabbath, and it is not lawful for you to carry your mat." [11] He answered them, "The man who made me well told me, 'Take up your mat and walk.' " [12] They asked him, "Who is the man who told you, 'Take it up and walk'?" [13] The man who was healed did not know who it was, for Jesus had slipped away, since there was a crowd there. [14] After this Jesus found him in the temple area and said to him, "Look, you are well; do not sin any more, so that nothing worse may happen to you." [15] The man went and told the Jews that Jesus was the one who had made him well.

This, the third sign in John's Gospel, differs from the two signs of Cana in that it is followed in verses 16–47 by a long dialogue or discourse. While this third sign may differ in style from those that occurred during the wedding feast at Cana (2:1–12) and in Galilee with the royal official's son (4:43–54), it resembles signs of the multiplication of the loaves and the fish (6:1–15) and the cure of the man who had been blind from birth (9:1–12), both of which are also followed by dialogues. It also resembles the seventh sign, the raising of Lazarus (11:1–44), which has dialogue dispersed throughout it. Barnabas Lindars offers the useful explanation that these dialogues were developed in the sermons and homilies of members of the Johannine community as they reflected on the meaning of Jesus' signs and as they moved further and further away from their roots in the Jewish synagogue.

In the passage at hand look carefully at the wording of 5:1: "[T]here was a feast of the Jews, and Jesus went up to Jerusalem." While the name of the feast is left unspecified, it is described as "of the Jews." Now this wording is strange since the author of the Fourth Gospel presumably was a Jew, Jesus was a Jew, and Jesus' first disciples were Jews. The phrase, "the Jews," refers to a group against which the Johannine community stands in contrast. It refers also to the Jewish religious authorities who object to Jesus' healing on a Sabbath (9). Against them Jesus preaches the sermon that follows this episode, in verses 16–47. Moreover, in the passage at hand the man who has been healed speaks of "the man who made me well" (11) and is referred to as "the man who was cured" (10) and "the man who was healed" (13). The Jewish authorities don't care that he was healed. Their issue is his having violated the Sabbath, and who is behind such a breach of God's law (11–12).

It is tempting to contrast the response of the man born blind (chapter 9) with the actions of this man at the Bethesda pool. The man born blind parries the questions of the religious leaders and grows in his faith in Jesus, whereas the man in this passage doesn't challenge the Jewish authorities and doesn't seem to grow in faith. But to compare one to the other is like comparing the brilliant attorney St. Thomas More (the man born blind) to ordinary Christians who try to make sense of God's dealings in their lives. The key to the representative character of the man in this passage is found in verses 10 to 15, especially the last statement: "The man went and told the Jews that Jesus was the one *who had made him well*" [italics added]. He doesn't say that Jesus told him to violate the Sabbath, but reiterates the fact that has changed his life: Jesus made him well. Thus, this man is an exemplary representative character. It is not his fault that the religious leaders refuse to hear his testimony: "Jesus healed me." He is busy trying to create a new life for himself.

A pattern emerges in the Fourth Gospel's narration of Jesus' signs. They are not the familiar "ordinary" miracles found in the Synoptics. Jesus does not provide a glass or two of common table wine, but fifty cases of premium wine. Jesus heals a child near death, but does so at a distance of some twenty-three miles. The man in this passage had been ill not for twelve years (see Mark 5:25) or eighteen years (see Luke 13:11). Rather he had been sick for thirty-eight years. Considering that life expectancy at the time of Jesus was at most forty, this man seems to have been ill his entire lifetime. The Evangelist, however, does not present Jesus' signs as flashy gestures. As Jesus will say later in 5:36: "The works that the Father gave me to accomplish, these works that I perform testify on my behalf that the Father has sent me." These signs reveal the Father's desire to bestow life on every member of the human family.

John 5:16–47: Jesus, the Son of God, Puts the Religious Authorities On Trial

[16] Therefore, the Jews began to persecute Jesus because he did this on a sabbath. [17] But Jesus answered them, "My Father is at work until now, so I am at work." [18] For this reason the Jews tried all the more to kill him, because he not only broke the sabbath but he also called God his own father, making himself equal to God.

[19] Jesus answered and said to them, "Amen, amen, I say to you, a son cannot do anything on his own, but only what he sees his father doing; for what he does, his son will do also. [20] For the Father loves his Son and shows him everything that he himself does, and he will show him greater works than these, so that you may be amazed. [21] For just as the Father raises the dead and gives life, so also does the Son give life to whomever he wishes. [22] Nor does the Father judge anyone, but he has given all judgment to his Son, [23] so that all may honor the Son just as they honor the Father. Whoever does not honor the Son does not honor the Father who sent him. [24] Amen, amen, I say to you, whoever hears my word and believes in the one who sent me has eternal life and will not come to condemnation, but has passed from death

to life. 25 Amen, amen, I say to you, the hour is coming and is now here when the dead will hear the voice of the Son of God, and those who hear will live. 26 For just as the Father has life in himself, so also he gave to his Son the possession of life in himself. 27 And he gave him power to exercise judgment, because he is the Son of Man. 28 Do not be amazed at this, because the hour is coming in which all who are in the tombs will hear his voice 29 and will come out, those who have done good deeds to the resurrection of life, but those who have done wicked deeds to the resurrection of condemnation.

30 "I cannot do anything on my own; I judge as I hear, and my judgment is just, because I do not seek my own will but the will of the one who sent me.

31 "If I testify on my own behalf, my testimony cannot be verified. 32 But there is another who testifies on my behalf, and I know that the testimony he gives on my behalf is true. 33 You sent emissaries to John, and he testified to the truth. 34 I do not accept testimony from a human being, but I say this so that you may be saved. 35 He was a burning and shining lamp, and for a while you were content to rejoice in his light. 36 But I have testimony greater than John's. The works that the Father gave me to accomplish, these works that I perform testify on my behalf that the Father has sent me. 37 Moreover, the Father who sent me has testified on my behalf. But you have never heard his voice nor seen his form, 38 and you do not have his word remaining in you, because you do not believe in the one whom he has sent. 39 You search the scriptures, because you think you have eternal life through them; even they testify on my behalf. 40 But you do not want to come to me to have life.

41 "I do not accept human praise; 42 moreover, I know that you do not have the love of God in you. 43 I came in

the name of my Father, but you do not accept me; yet if another comes in his own name, you will accept him. [44] How can you believe, when you accept praise from one another and do not seek the praise that comes from the only God? [45] Do not think that I will accuse you before the Father: the one who will accuse you is Moses, in whom you have placed your hope. [46] For if you had believed Moses, you would have believed me, because he wrote about me. [47] But if you do not believe his writings, how will you believe my words?"

Matthew, Mark, and Luke contain what scholars call "an implicit Christology," that is, Jesus' miracles point to his relationship to the Father. For example, in Luke 11:20 — "But if it is by the finger of God that [I] drive out demons, then the kingdom of God has come upon you" — Jesus is presented as the agent of God's kingdom. John's Gospel makes explicit what in the Synoptics is implicit: Jesus is God's Son. In the passage at hand the Fourth Evangelist presents a discourse by Jesus that plumbs the depths of what the sign of 5:1–15 (the cure at the Bethesda pool) only implies. But this discourse is extraordinary because it uses the terminology of a trial. In its first section, 16–30, the words "to judge" and "judgment" are prominent while in its second section, 31–47, the terms "to give witness" and "testimony" dominate. Although "the Jews" think that they are persecuting or prosecuting Jesus (16), it is they who are on trial, who are being judged, and the judge is Jesus.

The key verses of the first section are 19 and 17. When Jesus says, "Amen, amen, I say to you, a son cannot do anything on his own, but only what he sees his father doing; for what he does, his son will do also" (19), he is not making himself equal to God as the Jews accused him of doing (see verse 18). As God's Son, Jesus *is* equal to God. Verse 17 reads: "Jesus answered them, 'My Father is at work until now, so I am at work.' " In his discourse Jesus touches upon Jewish theological speculation of that era about what works God continues to do even during the Sabbath rest. God not only continues to sustain creation, but is also life-giver and judge. Even though the commandment prescribes Sabbath rest, children are born and thus given new life on the Sabbath; women and men die on the Sabbath and are subject to God's judgment. In the realized eschatology of the Fourth Gospel the judgment expected at the end of time is already present in the person of God's Son, Jesus. This judgment is either for life or for condemnation. The most powerful statement of this reality occurs in verse 24, which is often used in funeral liturgies: "Amen, amen, I say to you, whoever hears my word and believes in the one who sent me has eternal life and will not come to condemnation, but has passed from death to life." It is notable that verse 30, which concludes this portion of Jesus' discourse, includes the words "judge" and "judgment": "I cannot do anything on my own; I judge as I hear, and my judgment is just, because I do not seek my own will but the will of the one who sent me."

This discourse contains a dramatic irony: the religious authorities think that they are prosecuting Jesus, but readers of this Gospel realize that in fact the authorities themselves are being judged for their lack of faith. They cannot or will not look beyond Jesus' apparent violation of the Sabbath to the fact that Jesus had given new life to someone whose life had been impaired for thirty-eight years. This section of Jesus' sermon buoys up all those who feel persecuted or prosecuted, and foreshadows Jesus' raising of Lazarus, who hears Jesus' voice and comes forth from his tomb (see 5:28–29 and 11:43–44).

The second section, 31–47, must be read against the background of Deuteronomy 19:15: "[A] judicial fact shall be established only on the testimony of two or three witnesses." The Evangelist emphasizes this point by repeating "to witness" or "witness" eleven times in this section. Jesus is testifying only by himself. His Father also bears witness to him (32, 37–38), as does John the Witness (33–35). Works such as the healing performed at the Bethesda pool bear witness to Jesus. Scripture itself provides testimony about Jesus (39). Finally, even Moses gives testimony about Jesus, who thereby can accuse the religious leaders: "[I]f you do not believe his writings, how will you believe my words?" (47). Following Jesus' next sign, the multiplication of the loaves and the fishes, there is a discourse in which Jesus speaks again of how his signs complete those of Moses (see 6:30-34).

Although this trial scene may have initially stemmed, as Barnabas Lindars suggests, from Johannine polemic against the Jewish synagogue, it now stands as a bold proclamation of faith in Jesus as God's Son, as the One who gives life and judges, the one to whom many witnesses have pointed. Will contemporary Christians find comfort for their faith in the testimony of these witnesses? Will contemporary Christians find support for their faith that Jesus has already pronounced the sentence of eternal life upon them?

IV

Third Galilee/Jerusalem Cycle (6:1–10:42)

John 6:1–15: By Providing Abundant Food for People, Jesus Shows That He Is King

¹ After this, Jesus went across the Sea of Galilee [of Tiberias]. ² A large crowd followed him, because they saw the signs he was performing on the sick. ³ Jesus went up on the mountain, and there he sat down with his disciples. ⁴ The Jewish feast of Passover was near. ⁵ When Jesus raised his eyes and saw that a large crowd was coming to him, he said to Philip, "Where can we buy enough food for them to eat?" ⁶ He said this to test him, because he himself knew what he was going to do. ⁷ Philip answered him, "Two hundred days' wages worth of food would not be enough for each of them to have a little [bit]." ⁸ One of his disciples, Andrew, the brother of Simon Peter, said to him, ⁹ "There is a boy here who has five barley loaves and two fish; but what good are these for so many?" ¹⁰ Jesus said, "Have the people recline." Now there was a great deal of grass in that place. So the men reclined, about five thousand in number. ¹¹ Then Jesus took the loaves, gave thanks, and distributed them to those who were reclining, and also as much of the fish as they wanted. ¹² When they had had their fill, he said to his disciples, "Gather the fragments left over, so that nothing will be wasted." ¹³ So they collected them, and filled twelve wicker baskets with fragments from the five barley loaves that had been more than they could eat. ¹⁴ When the people saw the

sign he had done, they said, "This is truly the Prophet, the one who is to come into the world." [15] Since Jesus knew that they were going to come and carry him off to make him king, he withdrew again to the mountain alone.

By the time they encounter yet another gospel account of Jesus' multiplication of loaves some readers might say, "We've seen one. We've seen them all." Recall how many accounts there are: Matthew 14:13–21; Mark 6:32–44; Mark 8:1–9; Luke 9:10–17. But John's account has many unique features. Jesus is on a mountain (3). The Jewish Feast of Passover is just around the corner (4). Jesus initiates the action, even though there is no mention that the people are hungry (5–6). Two hundred days' wages could not buy enough to feed the people (7). Philip and Andrew are involved (7–9). The verb "recline" is used three times (10–11). Jesus, not his disciples, distributes the barley loaves (11). Jesus desires that "nothing be wasted" (12). The crowd hails Jesus as the Prophet (14) and would like to make him king (15).

These features are unique to John's account work on at least two levels. Some point ahead to the discourse that will follow in 6:26–58. "Mountain" and "Passover" should remind readers of Moses; on a mountain he received God's law, which represented God's food for the people. "Passover" recalls Moses leading the chosen people out of the slavery of Egypt and God feeding his people with manna as they trekked through the desert to the Promised Land. In 6:32 Jesus specifically invokes Moses, who was instrumental in providing it ("[I]t was not Moses who gave the bread from heaven; my Father gives you the true bread from heaven") and had earlier referred to Moses in 5:45–47. The

words "the Prophet" may echo Moses' words in Deuteronomy 18:15: "A prophet like me will the LORD, your God,
raise up for you from among your own kinsmen." The
phrase "so that nothing will be wasted" finds a counterpart
in 6:27: "Do not work for food that perishes."

The people's proposal to make him king shows that they
see the implications of what Jesus has done in this sign. Only
a Roman emperor had the power and the wealth to feed the
citizens abundantly. Although Jesus supplies the five thousand with food that poor people ate, even such a meager
meal does not come cheaply. "Two hundred days' wages"
for a minimum-wage worker today would come to over
$9,000. In Jesus' time, even for poor people who earned a
denarius a day, this simple meal came at a lavish cost.
Unlike the emperors, who had legions of minions to distribute their food to the citizens, Jesus distributes his food by
himself. On a literal level this seems difficult if not impossi-
ble, for had Jesus taken a mere five seconds with each
person, he would have needed seven hours to distribute the
loaves and fish. In the context of John's Christology, however, this means that Jesus, and Jesus alone, provides the
food that nourishes. Envision the five thousand from all
walks of life, clean and unclean, saints and sinners, reclining
festively on a hillside, not looking so much at one another as
at Jesus, the provider of their banquet of barley loaves. As
a counterimage, consider Statius' poetic depiction of
Emperor Domitian's Saturnalia Feast at Rome's Colosseum
(*Silvae* I.6). The eyes of the fifty thousand in attendance
were focused on Domitian, who provided rare fruits and
nuts from his far-flung empire, thus demonstrating
his power to supply choice and abundant food for his
people.

In John 2:1–12 the Evangelist had proclaimed via his first sign of overflowing choice wine that Jesus gives an abundance of life. Now he uses bread, the staple of life in the ancient world, to confess that Jesus gives life in superabundance. In 6:26–58 a preacher in the Johannine community takes this sign to a deeper level and explains that Jesus' teaching is food for life and that Jesus himself, whose flesh was broken and blood poured out on the cross, is food for eternal life.

John 6:16–21: Jesus Gets His Journeying Disciples Home in a Flash

> [16] When it was evening, his disciples went down to the sea, [17]embarked in a boat, and went across the sea to Capernaum. It had already grown dark, and Jesus had not yet come to them. [18] The sea was stirred up because a strong wind was blowing. [19] When they had rowed about three or four miles, they saw Jesus walking on the sea and coming near the boat, and they began to be afraid. [20] But he said to them, "It is I. Do not be afraid." [21] They wanted to take him into the boat, but the boat immediately arrived at the shore to which they were heading.

Mark 6:45–52 and Matthew 14:22–27 contain similar accounts; Matthew continues in verses 28–33 to narrate Peter's attempt to walk on water. Many commentators skip over this episode to concentrate on what they consider more substantial, Jesus' discourse on the bread of life. Yet this fourth sign is significant, especially if read from the disciples' perspective.

In their journey across the lake the disciples encounter some difficulty, but they are in no danger of perishing.

Walking on the water, Jesus comes to them. This is the same Jesus who in the three previous signs had provided abundant wine and bread, who had given new life to a man ill for thirty-eight years. The praise of God in Psalm 77:20 suggests the depth of this sign: "Through the sea was your path;/ your way, through the mighty waters...." Job 9:8 says: "[God] alone stretches out the heavens/ and treads upon the crests of the sea." The words Jesus uses when he reveals himself to his disciples, "It is I," can be taken on two levels. Literally, he is saying: "It's me. It's OK. Don't be alarmed." On a figurative level what Jesus says echoes God's words in Exodus 3:14, "I am who am," and in Isaiah 41:4, "I, the LORD, am the first,/ and with the last I will also be." In 41:10 Isaiah continues: "Fear not, I am with you;/ be not dismayed; I am your God." Jesus reveals himself only to his disciples, perhaps as preparation for his further revelation of himself as the bread of life, which many disciples will find hard to accept (see 6:60).

Only John's account contains the fact stated in verse 21: "They wanted to take him into the boat, but the boat immediately arrived at the shore to which they were heading." Perhaps this strange event has a rational explanation — in their confusion the disciples may not have realized how close to shore they actually were when Jesus approached them. But in a Gospel that deals so much with journeying, it seems more plausible that verse 21 narrates a sign within a sign. When Jesus is journeying with his disciples, they are able to reach home safely and quickly. How often might we find ourselves in the disciples' boat?

John 6:22–59: In Word and Sacrament
Jesus Is the Bread of Life

[22] The next day, the crowd that remained across the sea saw that there had been only one boat there, and that Jesus had not gone along with his disciples in the boat, but only his disciples had left. [23] Other boats came from Tiberias near the place where they had eaten the bread when the Lord gave thanks. [24] When the crowd saw that neither Jesus nor his disciples were there, they themselves got into boats and came to Capernaum looking for Jesus. [25] And when they found him across the sea they said to him, "Rabbi, when did you get here?" [26] Jesus answered them and said, "Amen, amen, I say to you, you are looking for me not because you saw signs but because you ate the loaves and were filled. [27] Do not work for food that perishes but for the food that endures for eternal life, which the Son of Man will give you. For on him the Father, God, has set his seal." [28] So they said to him, "What can we do to accomplish the works of God?" [29] Jesus answered and said to them, "This is the work of God, that you believe in the one he sent." [30] So they said to him, "What sign can you do, that we may see and believe in you? What can you do? [31] Our ancestors ate manna in the desert, as it is written: 'He gave them bread from heaven to eat.' " [32] So Jesus said to them, "Amen, amen, I say to you, it was not Moses who gave the bread from heaven; my Father gives you the true bread from heaven. [33] For the bread of God is that which comes down from heaven and gives life to the world."

[34] So they said to him, "Sir, give us this bread always." [35] Jesus said to them, "I am the bread of life; whoever comes to me will never hunger, and whoever believes in me will never thirst. [36] But I told you that although you

have seen [me], you do not believe. ³⁷ Everything that the Father gives me will come to me, and I will not reject anyone who comes to me, ³⁸ because I came down from heaven not to do my own will but the will of the one who sent me. ³⁹ And this is the will of the one who sent me, that I should not lose anything of what he gave me, but that I should raise it [on] the last day. ⁴⁰ For this is the will of my Father, that everyone who sees the Son and believes in him may have eternal life, and I shall raise him [on] the last day."

⁴¹ The Jews murmured about him because he said, "I am the bread that came down from heaven," ⁴² and they said, "Is this not Jesus, the son of Joseph? Do we not know his father and mother? Then how can he say, 'I have come down from heaven'?" ⁴³ Jesus answered and said to them, "Stop murmuring among yourselves. ⁴⁴ No one can come to me unless the Father who sent me draw him, and I will raise him on the last day. ⁴⁵ It is written in the prophets: 'They shall all be taught by God.' Everyone who listens to my Father and learns from him comes to me. ⁴⁶ Not that anyone has seen the Father except the one who is from God; he has seen the Father. ⁴⁷ Amen, amen, I say to you, whoever believes has eternal life. ⁴⁸ I am the bread of life. ⁴⁹ Your ancestors ate the manna in the desert, but they died; ⁵⁰ this is the bread that comes down from heaven so that one may eat it and not die. ⁵¹ I am the living bread that came down from heaven; whoever eats this bread will live forever; and the bread that I will give is my flesh for the life of the world."

⁵² The Jews quarreled among themselves, saying, "How can this man give us [his] flesh to eat?" ⁵³ Jesus said to them, "Amen, amen, I say to you, unless you eat the flesh of the Son of Man and drink his blood, you do not have life within you. ⁵⁴ Whoever eats my flesh and drinks my blood has eternal life, and I will raise him on

the last day. [55] For my flesh is true food, and my blood is true drink. [56] Whoever eats my flesh and drinks my blood remains in me and I in him. [57] Just as the living Father sent me and I have life because of the Father, so also the one who feeds on me will have life because of me. [58] This is the bread that came down from heaven. Unlike your ancestors who ate and still died, whoever eats this bread will live forever." [59] These things he said while teaching in the synagogue in Capernaum.

The meaning of this rich discourse and dialogue given in the synagogue at Capernaum (59) is best penetrated by considering it a sermon on the text quoted from the Law (Exodus 16:4, 15) in verse 31: "He gave them bread from heaven to eat." In his sermon Jesus demonstrates how Moses points to him (see 5:39–47). While there is considerable overlap between sections, verses 32–40 primarily interpret the words "he gave them." Verses 41–50 provide an exposition of "bread from heaven," and verses 51–58 explore the meaning of "to eat." Since sermons at that time used one text from the Law and one from the prophets, Jesus quotes Isaiah 54:13 in verse 45. Furthermore, sermons at that time brought in other biblical passages on the same basic theme, so this one too contains echoes of other sacred texts.

Note how verses 32–33 interpret the sermon theme of verse 31: "It was not Moses who gave the bread from heaven; my Father *gives* [not "gave"] *you* [not "them"] the *true* bread from heaven. For the bread of God is that which comes down from heaven and gives life to the world" (emphasis added). Indeed, as Jesus says, he is the bread of life, but only because he has been sent by his Father and does his Father's will. He gives true life, that is, eternal life, and will raise up on the last day those who believe in him (40).

The "murmuring" of verses 41–43 echoes Exodus 16:12, which describes the unhappiness of the Israelites in the desert and God's gift of manna: "I [God] have heard the grumbling of the Israelites. Tell them … in the morning you shall have your fill of bread, so that you may know that I, the LORD, am your God." "The Jews" misunderstand Jesus' origin (42) as earthly and fail to be taught by God. Verse 45 ("It is written in the prophets.… ") alludes to Isaiah 54:13: "All your sons shall be taught by the LORD." Traditionally, Israel saw the gift of manna as a sign of God's word and Torah. In Deuteronomy 8:3 Moses says: "He [God] therefore let you be afflicted with hunger, and then fed you with manna, a food unknown to you and your fathers, in order to show you that not by bread alone does man live, but by every word that comes forth from the mouth of the LORD." In Sirach 24:20–22, Wisdom herself states: "He who eats of me will hunger still,/ he who drinks of me will thirst for more.…/ All this is true of the book of the Most High's covenant,/ the law which Moses commanded us." Thus, Jesus, not the Law or Wisdom, is the bread of life for his current listeners (and readers), because the Israelite ancestors, who ate the manna, are dead. Jesus "is the bread that comes down from heaven so that one may eat it and not die" (50).

Although verse 50 had already introduced the notion of eating, verses 51–58 provide a more developed, eucharistic exposition. Some readers are bothered because the account of the Last Supper in John's Gospel (chapter 13) does not include the institution of the Eucharist. Yet a close reading of verses such as 6:51b indicate that the Johannine community knew of the words of institution: "[T]he bread that I will give is my flesh for the life of the world." Compare that verse with Luke 22:19: "This is my body, which will be given for you." John 6:52–56 stresses drinking Jesus' blood, as in verse 54: "Whoever eats my flesh and drinks my blood has eternal life." Compare this with Luke 22:20: "This cup is the new covenant in my blood, which will be shed for you." Indeed, verses 51–58 make it clear that Jesus will shed his blood for the life of the world.

Some preachers have problems with the 17th to the 21st Sundays of Liturgical Cycle B, which depart from Mark's Gospel and offer in its place chapter 6 of John. They feel constrained to preparing a homily on the Eucharist for five straight Sundays. But a careful reading reveals a number of other themes in the 71 verses of John 6, such as the scriptures as God's word or Jesus' power to give eternal life. They could question the contemporary agricultural economy that renders food a commodity upon which to earn profit instead of God's gift for the life of the world. They could challenge their congregations to ask themselves whether they love Jesus as much as a mother who lovingly says to her child: "I love you so much that I could eat you all up." Do we love Jesus deeply enough to eat up his revelation and to consume his love that spent itself for the life of the world?

John 6:60–71: Some Abandon Their Journey with Jesus and His Disciples

60 Then many of his disciples who were listening said, "This saying is hard; who can accept it?" 61 Since Jesus knew that his disciples were murmuring about this, he said to them, "Does this shock you? 62 What if you were to see the Son of Man ascending to where he was before? 63 It is the spirit that gives life, while the flesh is of no

avail. The words I have spoken to you are spirit and life. [64] But there are some of you who do not believe." Jesus knew from the beginning the ones who would not believe and the one who would betray him. [65] And he said, "For this reason I have told you that no one can come to me unless it is granted him by my Father."

[66] As a result of this, many [of] his disciples returned to their former way of life and no longer accompanied him. [67] Jesus then said to the Twelve, "Do you also want to leave?" [68] Simon Peter answered him, "Master, to whom shall we go? You have the words of eternal life. [69] We have come to believe and are convinced that you are the Holy One of God." [70] Jesus answered them, "Did I not choose you twelve? Yet is not one of you a devil?" [71] He was referring to Judas, son of Simon the Iscariot; it was he who would betray him, one of the Twelve.

The discourse and dialogue in John 6:31–58 mentions the crowds and "the Jews" murmuring. Now Jesus' own disciples are murmuring (61). On one level it is difficult to figure out who these disciples were historically, because they are distinct from the Twelve and "the Jews." Moreover, the boat on which they were journeying in 6:16–21 could hardly hold more than twenty people. On another level, however, these disciples are contemporary hearers of Jesus' sermon who find it "hard." What aspects of the sermon are hard? Perhaps all of them: Jesus, son of Joseph, is the bread that has come down from heaven; Jesus' teaching is better fare than God's Law and Wisdom; Jesus reveals God in the sacrificial giving of his flesh and the outpouring of his blood for the life of the world.

The gift of the Spirit enables the disciples who continue their journey with Jesus to see beyond the human plane and rejoice in the life-giving hard teaching and life of Jesus, the bread of life. Peter, who rarely is given a central position in John's Gospel, professes that Jesus is "the Holy One of God," the one set apart by the Father, the one who has the words of eternal life (68–69). For the moment the Twelve are steadfast, but by mentioning Judas, the Evangelist hints that on their journey with Jesus still harder times lie ahead.

Matthew 5–7 has its Sermon on the Mount and Luke 6 has its Sermon on the Plain. Both contain hard sayings of Jesus such as "love your enemies" (Matthew 5:44; Luke 6:27) that should separate true believers from half-hearted ones. Jesus' discourse in John 6:31–58 contains hard sayings that separate believers in Jesus as the bread of life from those who see him as nothing more than "the son of Joseph." Do Jesus' hard sayings put you into or outside his camp?

John 7:1–52: Jesus Provides the Living Water for the Feast of Tabernacles

¹ After this, Jesus moved about within Galilee; but he did not wish to travel in Judea, because the Jews were trying to kill him. ² But the Jewish feast of Tabernacles was near. ³ So his brothers said to him, "Leave here and go to Judea, so that your disciples also may see the works you are doing. ⁴ No one works in secret if he wants to be known publicly. If you do these things, manifest yourself to the world." ⁵ For his brothers did not believe in him. ⁶ So Jesus said to them, "My time is not yet here, but the time is always right for you. ⁷ The world cannot hate you, but it hates me, because I testify to it that its works are evil. ⁸ You go up to the feast. I am not going up to this feast, because my time has not yet been fulfilled." ⁹ After he had said this, he stayed on in Galilee.

¹⁰ But when his brothers had gone up to the feast, he himself also went up, not openly but [as it were] in secret. ¹¹ The Jews were looking for him at the feast and saying, "Where is he?" ¹² And there was considerable murmuring about him in the crowds. Some said, "He is a good man," [while] others said, "No; on the contrary, he misleads the crowd." ¹³ Still, no one spoke openly about him because they were afraid of the Jews.

¹⁴ When the feast was already half over, Jesus went up into the temple area and began to teach. ¹⁵ The Jews were amazed and said, "How does he know scripture without having studied?" ¹⁶ Jesus answered them and said, "My teaching is not my own but is from the one who sent me. ¹⁷ Whoever chooses to do his will shall know whether my teaching is from God or whether I speak on my own. ¹⁸ Whoever speaks on his own seeks his own glory, but whoever seeks the glory of the one who sent him is truthful, and there is no wrong in him. ¹⁹ Did not Moses give you the law? Yet none of you keeps the law. Why are you trying to kill me?" ²⁰ The crowd answered, "You are possessed! Who is trying to kill you?" ²¹ Jesus answered and said to them, "I performed one work and all of you are amazed ²² because of it. Moses gave you circumcision — not that it came from Moses but rather from the patriarchs — and you circumcise a man on the sabbath. ²³ If a man can receive circumcision on a sabbath so that the law of Moses may not be broken, are you angry with me because I made a whole person well on a sabbath? ²⁴ Stop judging by appearances, but judge justly."

²⁵ So some of the inhabitants of Jerusalem said, "Is he not the one they are trying to kill? ²⁶ And look, he is speaking openly and they say nothing to him. Could the authorities have realized that he is the Messiah? ²⁷ But we know where he is from. When the Messiah comes, no one will know where he is from." ²⁸ So Jesus cried out in the temple

area as he was teaching and said, "You know me and also know where I am from. Yet I did not come on my own, but the one who sent me, whom you do not know, is true. ²⁹ I know him, because I am from him, and he sent me." ³⁰ So they tried to arrest him, but no one laid a hand upon him, because his hour had not yet come. ³¹ But many of the crowd began to believe in him, and said, "When the Messiah comes, will he perform more signs than this man has done?"

³² The Pharisees heard the crowd murmuring about him to this effect, and the chief priests and the Pharisees sent guards to arrest him. ³³ So Jesus said, "I will be with you only a little while longer, and then I will go to the one who sent me. ³⁴ You will look for me but not find [me], and where I am you cannot come." ³⁵ So the Jews said to one another, "Where is he going that we will not find him? Surely he is not going to the dispersion among the Greeks to teach the Greeks, is he? ³⁶ What is the meaning of his saying, 'You will look for me and not find [me], and where I am you cannot come'?"

³⁷ On the last and greatest day of the feast, Jesus stood up and exclaimed, "Let anyone who thirsts come to me and drink. ³⁸ Whoever believes in me, as scripture says: 'Rivers of living water will flow from within him.' " ³⁹ He said this in reference to the Spirit that those who came to believe in him were to receive. There was, of course, no Spirit yet, because Jesus had not yet been glorified.

⁴⁰ Some in the crowd who heard these words said, "This is truly the Prophet." ⁴¹ Others said, "This is the Messiah." But others said, "The Messiah will not come from Galilee, will he? ⁴² Does not scripture say that the Messiah will be of David's family and come from Bethlehem, the village where David lived?" ⁴³ So a division occurred in the crowd because of him. ⁴⁴ Some of them even wanted to arrest him, but no one laid hands on him.

⁴⁵ So the guards went to the chief priests and Pharisees, who asked them, "Why did you not bring him?" ⁴⁶ The guards answered, "Never before has anyone spoken like this one." ⁴⁷ So the Pharisees answered them, "Have you also been deceived? ⁴⁸ Have any of the authorities or the Pharisees believed in him? ⁴⁹ But this crowd, which does not know the law, is accursed." ⁵⁰ Nicodemus, one of their members who had come to him earlier, said to them, "Does our law condemn a person before it first hears him and finds out what he is doing?"⁵² They answered and said to him, "You are not from Galilee also, are you? Look and see that no prophet arises from Galilee."

The first thirteen verses set the scene for what will transpire in the remainder of chapter 7 and all of chapter 8. In these two chapters Jesus proclaims that he himself replaces the Feast of Tabernacles, which commemorated and celebrated God's gifts of water and light. These chapters also contain much controversy. While the Synoptics generally assemble such controversies between Jesus and the religious leaders into neat blocks of material as Mark does in 2:1–3:6 and 11:1–12:44, John arranges them, as he does here and in chapter 8, in a somewhat disjointed fashion.

This episode follows a pattern John uses earlier in 2:3–10 (the wedding Feast at Cana), and 4:43–53 (healing the royal official's child). He uses it again in 11:3–15 (the raising of Lazarus): someone makes a suggestion to Jesus. At first Jesus rebuffs it, then eventually does what was suggested, but on his own terms. His kin, who do not believe in him (5), plead with Jesus to go to the Feast to make himself better known. Jesus rebuffs such an idea, but then goes up to the Feast of Tabernacles of his own accord. Verse 12 lays out the first controversy: "Some said, 'He is a good man,' [while] others said, 'No; on the contrary, he misleads the crowd.' " The charge that Jesus is misleading the people echoes Deuteronomy 13:13–16, which details how to deal with a person who may be misleading God's people by directing them to worship other gods. It begins: "If … you hear it said that certain scoundrels have sprung up among you and have led astray the inhabitants of their city to serve other gods whom you have not known...."

In many ways, what follows in 7:14–52 is a continuation of Jesus' trial in 5:16–47. Verse 18 of that earlier trial recounts how the Jews were trying to kill Jesus for breaking the Sabbath and making himself equal to God. In 7:19–24 Jesus argues that if it is lawful to circumcise a man on the Sabbath, it is lawful all the more to make a whole person well on a Sabbath. But this episode, unlike Jesus' earlier trial, includes voices other than those of the religious leaders. The people are divided in their opinions. Some think that Jesus is the Messiah, others do not. Some render their positive judgment on the basis of Jesus' works (31) or because never before has anyone spoken as he has (46). Others make their negative judgment because they think that they know Jesus' origins: "[W]e know where he is from. When the Messiah comes, no one will know where he is from" (27), and "The Messiah will not come from Galilee, will he?" (41). Despite three attempts by the people and the religious authorities to arrest Jesus (30, 32, 44) he remains free, for the hour when he will freely lay down his life has not yet come (7:30).

The trial aspect of 7:14–52 comes to a head in verses 45–52 when the Evangelist pits the religious authorities against one of their own, Nicodemus, and against two groups of marginalized people: the people who don't know

78

the law (49) and the Galileans (52). Nicodemus, one of the first representative characters in John's Gospel, stands up for Jesus by upholding the Law although his colleagues, supposed experts in the law, ignore it. His learned colleagues also fail to recall that the prophet Jonah came from Galilee (see 2 Kings 14:25). Ironically, those who claim to know the law — and so attack those with views concerning Jesus that differ from their own — display a lack of legal skill. It is also ironic that "the little people," unlearned in the law, are open to Jesus' revelation. As in the case of the Galilean royal official (4:43–54), Galileans, although not from the sophisticated big city of Jerusalem, have the honesty and openness to declare their faith in Jesus, the one sent from the Father.

Amid all this controversy Jesus makes a startling revelation: "Let anyone who thirsts come to me and drink. Whoever believes in me, as scripture says: 'Rivers of living water will flow from within him' " (37–38). The Feast of Tabernacles, which celebrates God's gift of water and thus of harvest, is being replaced by Jesus, who gives water. The Evangelist interprets this water to be Jesus' gift of the Spirit, to be given abundantly once Jesus had been glorified on the cross. Later, 19:34 describes the life-giving elements of blood and water that flowed from the pierced side of the crucified Jesus. Verses 37 to 39 echo Zechariah 14. At the end of time, when the LORD conquers, "living waters shall flow from Jerusalem" (8) and the nations shall come to Jerusalem to celebrate the Feast of Tabernacles (16), an event that resembles the speculation in 7:35 that Jesus is going to the "Greeks," that is, to the non-Jewish nations.

It's relatively easy to preach about the stories of the Samaritan woman and the man born blind, but the controversy in John 7–8 presents homilists with a particular challenge. Although John 7 may be hard to follow, some points are clear. Jesus is the water of life. For the most part, the religious leaders have already made up their minds against Jesus, but those considered ignorant of the Law, the Galileans, and Nicodemus approach Jesus' signs and teachings honestly, with open minds. The true heroes and heroines of the Johannine community include those ignorant of the Law, who kept turning over in their minds the evidence they had heard: "Never before has anyone spoken like this one." Often, the unerring, strong faith of "the little ones," those with little formal education, confounds learned doctors and pastors.

John 7:53–8:11: Jesus' Mercy for the Sinner Abounds

[53] Then each went to his own house, [8:1] while Jesus went to the Mount of Olives. [2] But early in the morning he arrived again in the temple area, and all the people started coming to him, and he sat down and taught them. [3] Then the scribes and the Pharisees brought a woman who had been caught in adultery and made her stand in the middle. [4] They said to him, "Teacher, this woman was caught in the very act of committing adultery. [5] Now in the law, Moses commanded us to stone such women. So what do you say?" [6] They said this to test him, so that they could have some charge to bring against him. Jesus bent down and began to write on the ground with his finger. [7] But when they continued asking him, he straightened up and said to them, "Let the one among you who is without sin be the first to throw a stone at her." [8] Again he bent down and wrote on the ground. [9] And in response, they went away one by one, beginning with the elders. So he was left alone with

80

the woman before him. [10] Then Jesus straightened up and said to her, "Woman, where are they? Has no one condemned you?" [11] She replied, "No one, sir." Then Jesus said, "Neither do I condemn you. Go, [and] from now on do not sin any more."

This passage does indeed disrupt the context, is poorly attested in the manuscript tradition, and contains words such as "the scribes" found nowhere else in John's Gospel; nevertheless, it is canonical scripture for Roman Catholics and occurs in the lectionary on the fifth Sunday of Lent for Cycle C. As already established, John 7–8 contains controversy upon controversy, so this controversial passage seems to fit right in. Yet if compared with controversies in the Synoptics, it seems more Synoptic than Johannine. That is, it deals more with interpretation of the Law, whereas Johannine controversies such as the others in John 7–8 are more profoundly Christological and focus on Jesus as the one sent by God.

This controversy has a twofold legal background. In the first place, as Deuteronomy 17:6 states, the death penalty requires not just one but two or three witnesses. Secondly, in prescribing the penalty for adultery, Deuteronomy 22:22 states: "If a man is discovered having relations with a woman who is married to another, both the man and the woman with whom he has had relations shall die. Thus shall you purge the evil from your midst." Contemporary feminist scholars raise questions that the text does not address: What has happened to the man caught in the very act of adultery? Has the husband entrapped her, secreting two witnesses in the bedroom as part of a conspiracy to act out of an unlawful double standard and let their male comrade escape judgment? Is Jesus' action blameless in solving the moral dilemma thrown into his lap? After all, he does use the woman's life as bait. In John's Gospel Jesus is portrayed as knowing all things, but this story does not show him using his omniscience. Instead, he seems to hope that the religious leaders will be conscience-struck and not stone the woman to death.

Jesus' response raises the clear challenge: Which of you has not violated the Law of God? The religious leaders, beginning with the eldest, leave the trial scene and do not carry out the execution of the woman. By doing so, they acknowledge that they, too, have violated God's Law. Is Jesus too lax? It seems not, for he tells the woman to sin no more. Mercy in the person of Jesus meets the sinful woman in her misery, and Jesus does not condemn her. Might the adulterous woman be a representative character? The Greek word in verse 11 translated as "sir" ("She replied, 'No one, sir' "), *Kyrie*, is usually translated as "Lord." The sinful woman is confessing her faith in Jesus, the merciful, the friend of tax collectors and sinners (Luke 7:34).

John 8:12–59: High Christology Soars Above Strident Polemic

[12] Jesus spoke to them again, saying, "I am the light of the world. Whoever follows me will not walk in darkness, but will have the light of life." [13] So the Pharisees said to him, "You testify on your own behalf, so your testimony cannot be verified." [14] Jesus answered and said to them, "Even if I do testify on my own behalf, my testi-

mony can be verified, because I know where I came from and where I am going. But you do not know where I come from or where I am going. [15] You judge by appearances, but I do not judge anyone. [16] And even if I should judge, my judgment is valid, because I am not alone, but it is I and the Father who sent me. [17] Even in your law it is written that the testimony of two men can be verified. [18] I testify on my behalf and so does the Father who sent me." [19] So they said to him, "Where is your father?" Jesus answered, "You know neither me nor my Father. If you knew me, you would know my Father also." [20] He spoke these words while teaching in the treasury in the temple area. But no one arrested him, because his hour had not yet come.

[21] He said to them again, "I am going away and you will look for me, but you will die in your sin. Where I am going you cannot come." [22] So the Jews said, "He is not going to kill himself, is he, because he said, 'Where I am going you cannot come'?" [23] He said to them, "You belong to what is below, I belong to what is above. You belong to this world, but I do not belong to this world. [24] That is why I told you that you will die in your sins. For if you do not believe that I AM, you will die in your sins." [25] So they said to him, "Who are you?" Jesus said to them, "What I told you from the beginning. [26] I have much to say about you in condemnation. But the one who sent me is true, and what I heard from him I tell the world." [27] They did not realize that he was speaking to them of the Father. [28] So Jesus said [to them], "When you lift up the Son of Man, then you will realize that I AM, and that I do nothing on my own, but I say only what the Father taught me. [29] The one who sent me is with me. He has not left me alone, because I always do what is pleasing to him." [30] Because he spoke this way, many came to believe in him.

³¹ Jesus then said to those Jews who believed in him, "If you remain in my word, you will truly be my disciples, ³² and you will know the truth, and the truth will set you free." ³³ They answered him, "We are descendants of Abraham and have never been enslaved to anyone. How can you say, 'You will become free'?" ³⁴ Jesus answered them, "Amen, amen, I say to you, everyone who commits sin is a slave of sin. ³⁵ A slave does not remain in a household forever, but a son always remains. ³⁶ So if a son frees you, then you will truly be free. ³⁷ I know that you are descendants of Abraham. But you are trying to kill me, because my word has no room among you. ³⁸ I tell you what I have seen in the Father's presence; then do what you have heard from the Father."

³⁹ They answered and said to him, "Our father is Abraham." Jesus said to them, "If you were Abraham's children, you would be doing the works of Abraham. ⁴⁰ But now you are trying to kill me, a man who has told you the truth that I heard from God; Abraham did not do this. ⁴¹ You are doing the works of your father!" [So] they said to him, "We are not illegitimate. We have one Father, God." ⁴² Jesus said to them, "If God were your Father, you would love me, for I came from God and am here; I did not come on my own, but he sent me. ⁴³ Why do you not understand what I am saying? Because you cannot bear to hear my word. ⁴⁴ You belong to your father the devil and you willingly carry out your father's desires. He was a murderer from the beginning and does not stand in truth, because there is no truth in him. When he tells a lie, he speaks in character, because he is a liar and the father of lies. ⁴⁵ But because I speak the truth, you do not believe me. ⁴⁶ Can any of you charge me with sin? If I am telling the truth, why do you not believe me? ⁴⁷ Whoever belongs to God hears the words

of God; for this reason you do not listen, because you do not belong to God."

⁴⁸ The Jews answered and said to him, "Are we not right in saying that you are a Samaritan and are possessed?" ⁴⁹ Jesus answered, "I am not possessed; I honor my Father, but you dishonor me. ⁵⁰ I do not seek my own glory; there is one who seeks it and he is the one who judges. ⁵¹ Amen, amen, I say to you, whoever keeps my word will never see death." ⁵² [So] the Jews said to him, "Now we are sure that you are possessed. Abraham died, as did the prophets, yet you say, 'Whoever keeps my word will never taste death.' ⁵³ Are you greater than our father Abraham, who died? Or the prophets, who died? Who do you make yourself out to be?" ⁵⁴ Jesus answered, "If I glorify myself, my glory is worth nothing; but it is my Father who glorifies me, of whom you say, 'He is our God.' ⁵⁵ You do not know him, but I know him. And if I should say that I do not know him, I would be like you a liar. But I do know him and I keep his word. ⁵⁶ Abraham your father rejoiced to see my day; he saw it and was glad." ⁵⁷ So the Jews said to him, "You are not yet fifty years old and you have seen Abraham?" ⁵⁸ Jesus said to them, "Amen, amen, I say to you, before Abraham came to be, I AM." ⁵⁹ So they picked up stones to throw at him; but Jesus hid and went out of the temple area.

The harsh exchange in this passage may seem off-putting, but that does not lessen the power and beauty of its high Christology. Although this is one of the most difficult passages in John's Gospel and preachers often avoid it, there are two points that may suggest some direction that help with interpreting it.

First, we are familiar with contemporary styles of argument and know how to interpret them, but for the most part we don't understand ancient polemic. The famous blasts of the prophets against their fellow Israelites provide a good example. Isaiah uses graphic imagery: "... you are stubborn/ ... your neck is an iron sinew/ and your forehead bronze" (48:4). He continues: "Yes, I know that you are utterly treacherous,/ a rebel you were called from birth" (48:8). Just as the Fourth Evangelist, in a sense, takes "the Jews" to court, so too does Hosea: "Hear the word of the LORD, O people of Israel,/ for the LORD has a grievance against the inhabitants of the land:/ There is no fidelity, no mercy,/ no knowledge of God in the land./ False swearing, lying, murder, stealing and adultery!/ in their lawlessness, bloodshed follows bloodshed" (4:1–2). John's Gospel shares the same exaggerated accusations that 1 Timothy 1:8–10 levels against its opponents: "We know that the law is good, provided that one uses it as law, with the understanding that law is meant not for a righteous person but for the lawless and unruly, the godless and sinful, the unholy and profane, those who kill their fathers or mothers, murderers, the unchaste, sodomites, kidnapers, liars, perjurers, and whatever else is opposed to sound teaching." The opponents whom Paul censures probably had not murdered their fathers and mothers or kidnaped anyone. It is the style of polemic to exaggerate so as to make one's opponents appear repugnant.

Contemporary public discourse often resembles the polemic of this passage. Some who dislike the United States say that America is so very bad that it is Satan. In political campaigns one opponent will demonize another. Some commentators, especially those with a religious agenda, even suggest that if so and so wins the presidential election, Satan will be residing at 1600 Pennsylvania Avenue. In verse 44 Jesus goes to the root of the problem of "the Jews": "You belong to your father the devil and you willingly carry out your father's desires. He was a murderer from the beginning and does not stand in truth, because there is no truth in him." For their part "the Jews" demonize Jesus: "The Jews answered and said to him, 'Are we not right in saying that you are a Samaritan and are possessed?' " "Possessed," they mean, with a demon.

Polemic is harsh and clever. It aims for total victory. That being so, it is important to note that this passage, especially verses 12–59, recounts an in-house, domestic dispute. It is not anti-Semitism. It is not anti-Judaism, for Jews are engaging in polemic against fellow Jews. This domestic quarrel is so fierce because the stakes are so high. The high Christology of verses 12–59 reveals just how high these stakes are.

A key aspect of John's high Christology occurs straight-away in verse 12: "Jesus spoke to them again, saying: 'I am the light of the world. Whoever follows me will not walk in darkness, but will have the light of life.' " John's Prologue already stated that the pre-existent Word was "[t]he true light, which enlightens everyone [and] was coming into the world" (1:9). Jesus reveals that he is the light of the world on the Feast of Tabernacles. The Mishnah, an interpretation of Jewish Law written about 200 AD, describes the ceremony of light celebrated at night during that same feast. A close paraphrase of Herbert Danby's translation of 5:2–3 reads: "There were golden candlesticks in the Court of the Women with four golden bowls on the top of them and four ladders to each candlestick, and four youths of the priestly stock and in their hands jars of oil holding twelve gallons which they poured into all the bowls. They made wicks from the worn-out drawers and girdles of the priests and with them they set the candlesticks alight, and there was not a courtyard in Jerusalem that did not reflect the light of the Beth ha-She'ubah." The lights of Tabernacles illumine all of Jerusalem, but Jesus replaces this feast of lights as he illumines the entire world. In chapter 9, John illustrates that Jesus is the light of the world with the story of Jesus' giving sight to a man born blind.

The Fourth Gospel has already shown that Jesus is the bread of life (6:48) and the light of the world (8:12). In the chapters that follow Jesus will also proclaim: "I am the gate for the sheep" (10:7); "I am the good shepherd" (10:11); "I am the resurrection and the life" (11:25); "I am the true vine" (15:1). In each of these statements, "I am" is linked with a predicate (bread, light, gate, shepherd, resurrection and life, true vine). In 8:12–59 we find three examples of "I am" without a predicate. As background for this extraordinary usage of "I am," see Exodus 3:13–14, where Moses asks, "When I go to the Israelites and say to them, 'The God of your fathers has sent me to you,' if they ask me, 'What is his name?' what am I to tell them?" and is told, " 'I am who am.' Then he added, 'This is what you shall tell the Israelites: I AM sent me to you.' " Closer to the time of John's Gospel, the Greek Septuagint version of Isaiah 41:4* says: "I, God, am the first, and with the last I AM." It is small wonder that there is a dispute between Jesus and "the Jews," for Jesus is calling himself God. In verse 24 he says, "[I]f you do not believe that I AM, you will die in your sins." Verse 28 adds to this high Christology that Jesus shows he is divine through his life-giving death on the cross: "When you lift up the Son of Man, then you will realize that I AM, and that I do nothing on my own, but I say only what the Father taught me." Finally, verse 58 proclaims unequivocally Jesus' pre-existence: "Amen, amen, I say to you, before Abraham came to be, I AM."

The harsh give-and-take of this passage need not blind readers to its vibrant Christology. In God's Temple, during the Feast of Water and Light, Jesus is proclaiming that he is water and light for the world. What Tabernacles celebrated, Jesus is. The Jews vigorously protest Jesus' claims to be I AM even to the point of trying to stone him (59). But it is not yet time for Jesus to lay down his life, to be lifted up on the cross, so that people may believe that he is I AM.

John 9:1–41: A Blind Beggar Is a Courageous Witness in and for the Johannine Community

[1] As he passed by he saw a man blind from birth. [2] His disciples asked him, "Rabbi, who sinned, this man or his parents, that he was born blind?" [3] Jesus answered, "Neither he nor his parents sinned; it is so that the works of God might be made visible through him. [4] We have to do the works of the one who sent me while it is day. Night is coming when no one can work. [5] While I am in the world, I am the light of the world." [6] When he had said this, he spat on the ground and made clay with the saliva, and smeared the clay on his eyes, [7] and said to him, "Go wash in the Pool of Siloam" (which means Sent). So he went and washed, and came back able to see.

[8] His neighbors and those who had seen him earlier as a beggar said, "Isn't this the one who used to sit and beg?" [9] Some said, "It is," but others said, "No, he just looks like

him." He said, "I am." ¹⁰ So they said to him, "[So] how were your eyes opened?" ¹¹ He replied, "The man called Jesus made clay and anointed my eyes and told me, 'Go to Siloam and wash.' So I went there and washed and was able to see." ¹² And they said to him, "Where is he?" He said, "I don't know."

¹³ They brought the one who was once blind to the Pharisees. ¹⁴ Now Jesus had made clay and opened his eyes on a sabbath. ¹⁵ So then the Pharisees also asked him how he was able to see. He said to them, "He put clay on my eyes, and I washed, and now I can see." ¹⁶ So some of the Pharisees said, "This man is not from God, because he does not keep the sabbath." [But] others said, "How can a sinful man do such signs?" And there was a division among them. ¹⁷ So they said to the blind man again, "What do you have to say about him, since he opened your eyes?" He said, "He is a prophet."

¹⁸ Now the Jews did not believe that he had been blind and gained his sight until they summoned the parents of the one who had gained his sight. ¹⁹ They asked them, "Is this your son, who you say was born blind? How does he now see?" ²⁰ His parents answered and said, "We know that this is our son and that he was born blind. ²¹ We do not know how he sees now, nor do we know who opened his eyes. Ask him, he is of age; he can speak for himself." ²² His parents said this because they were afraid of the Jews, for the Jews had already agreed that if anyone acknowledged him as the Messiah, he would be expelled from the synagogue. ²³ For this reason his parents said, "He is of age; question him."

²⁴ So a second time they called the man who had been blind and said to him, "Give God the praise! We know that this man is a sinner." ²⁵ He replied, "If he is a sinner, I do not know. One thing I do know is that I was blind and now I see." ²⁶ So they said to him, "What did he do to

you? How did he open your eyes?" 27 He answered them, "I told you already and you did not listen. Why do you want to hear it again? Do you want to become his disciples, too?" 28 They ridiculed him and said, "You are that man's disciple; we are disciples of Moses! 29 We know that God spoke to Moses, but we do not know where this one is from." 30 The man answered and said to them, "This is what is so amazing, that you do not know where he is from, yet he opened my eyes. 31 We know that God does not listen to sinners, but if one is devout and does his will, he listens to him. 32 It is unheard of that anyone ever opened the eyes of a person born blind. 33 If this man were not from God, he would not be able to do anything." 34 They answered and said to him, "You were born totally in sin, and are you trying to teach us?" Then they threw him out.

35 When Jesus heard that they had thrown him out, he found him and said, "Do you believe in the Son of Man?" 36 He answered and said, "Who is he, sir, that I may believe in him?" 37 Jesus said to him, "You have seen him and the one speaking with you is he." 38 He said, "I do believe, Lord," and he worshiped him. 39 Then Jesus said, "I came into this world for judgment, so that those who do not see might see, and those who do see might become blind."

40 Some of the Pharisees who were with him heard this and said to him, "Surely we are not also blind, are we?" 41 Jesus said to them, "If you were blind, you would have no sin; but now you are saying, 'We see,' so your sin remains."

Baptismal preparation classes and homilies may have rendered this story so familiar that readers do not examine it carefully. But looking at it from a variety of perspectives might allow them to see it with new eyes.

This sign, the sixth in John's Gospel, has parallels in the Gospel of Mark. In Mark 8:22–26 a blind man is brought to Jesus for healing. Jesus puts spittle on the man's eyes and has to touch these blind eyes twice before he can see perfectly. In Mark 10:45–52 the blind beggar, Bartimaeus, twice petitions Jesus, son of David, for healing. Jesus rewards the blind man's persistent begging by restoring his sight with a mere word. Bartimaeus then follows Jesus on the road. In the first story from Mark as well as in John 9, Jesus uses spittle. In Mark's second story of curing blindness and in this passage from John 9 the man healed becomes Jesus' disciple. John alone, however, has the cure occur on the Sabbath, portrays the man who is healed as blind from birth, and describes him being put on trial by "the Jews."

John places this event in the Temple area to illustrate what Jesus proclaimed during the Feast of Tabernacles: "I am the light of the world. Whoever follows me will not walk in darkness, but will have the light of life" (8:12). Furthermore, reading this story in the context of the entire Gospel of John reveals that in the next chapter it leads to Jesus' description of himself as the good shepherd (10:1–21). The cure of the man born blind introduces a powerful theme concerning the identity of the true shepherd. Is it the religious leaders, those who cast the man born blind from the synagogue, or is it Jesus? John 10:21 ("Surely a demon cannot open the eyes of the blind, can he?") reveals that in chapter 10 the Evangelist still has in mind events from chapter 9. Moreover, John's Gospel frequently has the figure of Moses appear, as in 1:17: "... while the law was given through Moses, grace and truth came through Jesus Christ" or in 5:46–47 when Jesus attacks "the Jews," proclaiming, "For if you had believed Moses, you would have believed me, because he wrote about me. But if you do not believe his writings, how will you believe my words?" This context provides a framework for understanding more deeply verses 28–29: "They ['the Jews'] ridiculed him and said, 'You are that man's disciple; we are disciples of Moses! We know that God spoke to Moses, but we do not know where this one is from.' " Baruch 4:1–2 illustrates the background of this charge against the man born blind, for the prophet equates wisdom with the law given through Moses and states that the law gives light. Baruch says: "She [wisdom] is the book of the precepts of God,/ the law that endures forever;/ All who cling to her will live,/ but those will die who forsake her./ Turn, O Jacob, and receive her:/ walk by her light toward splendor." Ironically, the man born blind sees because of the light of Jesus, light of the world, whereas the religious authorities acknowledge only one source of light, the law, and their interpretation of that law. When Jesus declares, "If you were blind, you would have no sin; but now you are saying, 'We see,' so your sin remains" (41), he asserts that their illumination is actually blindness.

The nature of the community for which the Gospel of John was written also provides a context for understanding this story. Many scholars find verse 22 a window into what was happening in John's community: "His parents said this because they were afraid of the Jews, for the Jews had already agreed that if anyone acknowledged him as the Messiah, he would be expelled from the synagogue." In verse 34, "the Jews" throw the man born blind out of the synagogue. Two other passages also echo verse 22: "Nevertheless, many, even among the authorities, believed in him, but because of the Pharisees they did not acknowledge it openly in order not to be expelled from the synagogue" (12:42); and 16:2, in which Jesus warns his disciples: "They will expel you from the synagogues...." The Christian Jews of John's community seem in the process of separating themselves or already have separated from their mother community, the Jewish synagogue, because of their belief in Jesus as the one sent from the Father. The bitter polemic in John 5, 7, and 8 stems from this painful separation. It is not important to focus attention on the conditions behind it, but on the representative character of the man born blind. Although not a theologian but only a beggar, a marginalized person, he stands up to the religious authorities, grows in his faith, and suffers the consequences of witnessing staunchly to what Jesus had done for him. Just as Jesus was put on trial after he cured the cripple at Bethesda, forgave the woman caught in adultery, and proclaimed his identity at the Feast of Tabernacles, so is the man born blind, who acquits himself very well, for he is "taught by God" (6:45).

The story itself consists of seven carefully crafted scenes: Jesus healing the man born blind (1–7); neighbors' questions (8–12); first inquisition by the religious authorities (13–16); the religious authorities questioning the parents (17–23); the second inquisition (24–34); Jesus revealing himself to the man (35–39); Jesus confronting the religious authorities (40–41). In these scenes the man born blind speaks ten times, most articulately during his second interrogation. His words reveal his growth in faith: Jesus is a prophet (17), Jesus has disciples (28), Jesus is from God (33), Jesus is the Son of Man (35), Jesus is Lord (38). Finally, the man who comes to see because of the light of Jesus worships him (38).

94

Another theme running through these scenes is that of sin. In verses 1–3 the disciples wonder whether sin has caused the man's blindness, as do "the Jews" in verse 34. In verse 16 the Pharisees question whether Jesus may be a sinner because he does not keep the Sabbath. However, can a sinful person do such signs? In verses 24–25 the religious authorities are convinced that since he did not observe the Sabbath Jesus is a sinner, but the man born blind refuses to engage in such discussion. Instead, he holds onto the one fact he knows: he couldn't see before, and now he can. In verse 31 he becomes a theologian: "We know that God does not listen to sinners, but if one is devout and does his will, he listens to him." By verse 41 the focus changes, for the sin in question is no longer violation of the Sabbath, but willful refusal to believe in Jesus: "Jesus said to them, 'If you were blind, you would have no sin; but now you are saying, "We see," so your sin remains.' " Ironically, the religious authorities think that they have tried the man born blind and condemned him to expulsion, but all along they themselves have been on trial.

Finally, two subtle expressions heighten the narrative Christology of this entire passage. Siloam, the name of pool to which Jesus sends the man born blind, means "Sent" (7). Jesus, sent from the Father, is the light of the world. Then, the religious leaders ask the man born blind to swear an oath: "Give God the praise" (24), echoing the book of Joshua: "Joshua said to Achan, 'My son, give the LORD, the God of Israel, glory and honor, by telling me what you have done; do not hide it from me' " (Jo 7:19). Their own blindness, ironically, prevents them from seeing that Jesus is the one who has come to give glory to God through being lifted up willingly on the cross for the life of the world. The man born blind truly sees the glory revealed in this sixth sign and worships Jesus.

Behind its familiar facts, this story contains challenging ideas. The man born blind is an outstanding character. The religious leaders fail to see who Jesus truly is, but this beggar, this person who lives on the margins of society, holds fast to what Jesus has done for him. In holding on to his experience, he deepens his faith in Jesus and in the end worships him. In Mark, Jesus says "Whoever has ears ought to hear" (Mk 4:9). Here, he could well say, "Whoever has eyes to see, ought to see."

John 10:1–21: Jesus Is the Gate for His Sheep and the Noble Shepherd

¹ "Amen, amen, I say to you, whoever does not enter a sheepfold through the gate but climbs over elsewhere is a thief and a robber. ² But whoever enters through the gate is the shepherd of the sheep. ³ The gatekeeper opens it for him, and the sheep hear his voice, as he calls his own sheep by name and leads them out. ⁴ When he has driven out all his own, he walks ahead of them, and the sheep follow him, because they recognize his voice. ⁵ But they will not follow a stranger; they will run away from him, because they do not recognize the voice of strangers." ⁶ Although Jesus used this figure of speech, they did not realize what he was trying to tell them.

⁷ So Jesus said again, "Amen, amen, I say to you, I am the gate for the sheep. ⁸ All who came [before me] are thieves and robbers, but the sheep did not listen to them. ⁹ I am the gate. Whoever enters through me will be saved, and will come in and go out and find pasture. ¹⁰ A thief comes only to steal and slaughter and destroy; I came so that they might have life and have it more abundantly.

[11] I am the good shepherd. A good shepherd lays down his life for the sheep. [12] A hired man, who is not a shepherd and whose sheep are not his own, sees a wolf coming and leaves the sheep and runs away, and the wolf catches and scatters them. [13] This is because he works for pay and has no concern for the sheep. [14] I am the good shepherd, and I know mine and mine know me, [15] just as the Father knows me and I know the Father; and I will lay down my life for the sheep. [16] I have other sheep that do not belong to this fold. These also I must lead, and they will hear my voice, and there will be one flock, one shepherd. [17] This is why the Father loves me, because I lay down my life in order to take it up again. [18] No one takes it from me, but I lay it down on my own. I have power to lay it down, and power to take it up again. This command I have received from my Father."

[19] Again there was a division among the Jews because of these words. [20] Many of them said, "He is possessed and out of his mind; why listen to him?" [21] Others said, "These are not the words of one possessed; surely a demon cannot open the eyes of the blind, can he?"

The events surrounding Jesus in Jerusalem during the Feast of Tabernacles that began in chapter 7 continue here. He has already taught and illustrated through the sign of giving sight to a man born blind that he has fulfilled the meaning of the Feast of Tabernacles, for he is life-giving water and the light of the world. This passage, part of Jesus' last discourse during his public ministry, develops a theme established in chapter 9: Jesus, not the religious leaders, is the true shepherd or leader of God's people. Verse 21 recalls the story of Jesus' cure of the man born blind in mind as the Evangelist writes: "Others said, 'These are not the words of one possessed; surely a demon cannot open the eyes of the blind, can he?' "

This discourse makes much more sense when viewed against its Old Testament background. David, Israel's leader and famous king, was a shepherd. Ezekiel 34 is a tirade against Israel's leaders, the shepherds, who fatten themselves rather than care for God's people, the sheep. Verses 2–4 read: "Thus says the Lord GOD: Woe to the shepherds of Israel who have been pasturing themselves! Should not shepherds, rather, pasture sheep? You have fed off their milk, worn their wool, and slaughtered the fatlings, but the sheep you have not pastured. You did not strengthen the weak nor heal the sick nor bind up the injured. You did not bring back the strayed nor seek the lost, but you lorded it over them harshly and brutally." In verse 10 God pronounces judgment against these selfish and unjust shepherds: "Thus says the Lord GOD: I swear I am coming against these shepherds. I will claim my sheep from them and put a stop to their shepherding my sheep so that they may no longer pasture themselves. I will save my sheep that they may no longer be food for their mouths." These passages elucidate what Jesus had in mind in referring to "thieves and robbers" (8), "a stranger" (5), or "a hired man" (12); they represent the antitype of a true shepherd.

The first ten verses of this passage form the gospel reading for the fourth Sunday after Easter in Cycle A, often called "Good Shepherd" Sunday. This perplexes some preachers, because the excerpt does not mention the Good Shepherd. Rather, John uses the metaphor of the gate: "Amen, amen, I say to you, I am the gate for the sheep…. I am the gate. Whoever enters through me will be saved, and will come in and go out and find pasture…. I came so that they might have life and have it more abundantly" (7–10). The image of Jesus as gate allows us to see that John's figures of speech often take the form of riddles that thoughtful readers puzzle over to extract their exact meaning and application. Earlier in this Gospel Jesus is described as living water, the bread of life, and light for the world, each a puzzling metaphor. What type of bread does Jesus supply? What must this living water taste like? How bright is the light of Jesus? The Evangelist prompts readers to not be satisfied with clichés. John's metaphors and riddles take readers beyond the limits of words to see, touch, taste and hear the reality that is Jesus. In the instance at hand Jesus is the gate through which believers pass to find salvation. Think of what gates do. Think of gated communities. Think of gates that slam shut on prisoners. Think of the pearly gates. Once, the gate to my 10 p.m. flight was already closed, but the agent radioed the pilot and got permission to open it for me, saving me from an uncomfortable night in the Newark airport. Make John's metaphors and riddles your own, remembering as you do so that images change to fit the experience of the person interpreting them. By imagining them anew, they remain ever fresh. Indeed, Jesus is the gate that swings open, allowing believers to enter into more abundant life.

In verses 11–18 the title given to Jesus is generally translated as "*good* shepherd," but in Greek the adjective is *kalos,* rendered more accurately in English as "noble." In choosing the proper way to translate a term, it is sometimes useful to examine a word in terms of its opposite. The antonym of "good" is "evil," but the antonym of "noble" is "shameful" or "disgraceful." John's Gospel frequently mentions "glory," be it what the Jews who seek their own glory and honor are pursuing, or what Jesus who seeks the Father's glory pursues. For example, in 8:50 Jesus says: "I do not seek my own glory." "Noble" belongs to this universe of discourse, namely, that of honor and shame. It is also useful to recall the threefold leitmotif that runs through verses 11–18: Jesus *freely* gives up his life *for his sheep* and *takes it up again*. Thus, Jesus is a noble shepherd because for the sake of others he voluntarily gives up his life and is not vanquished by death. Had he not done these three things, he would be not the evil shepherd, but the disgraceful shepherd.

This Greek tradition of a noble death finds expression in Jewish literature that celebrates the courageous death of Eleazar, as well as those of the mother and her seven sons during the reign of Antiochus Epiphanes IV, who desecrated the Jerusalem Temple and forced Jews to defile themselves by eating pork and so deny their God. Passages from the books of the Maccabees that recount these events provide useful background for the next feast that John mentions (10:22-39), the celebration of the rededication of the Temple. The Second Book of Maccabees 6:19 praises Eleazar, who refusing to eat pork goes to his torture and death: "But preferring a glorious death to a life of defilement, he spat out the meat, and went forward of his own accord to the instrument of torture." An apocryphal treatise from the first century AD, 4 Maccabees, celebrates the deaths of the mother and her seven sons: "These, then, having consecrated themselves for the sake of God, are now honored not only with this distinction but also by the fact that through them our enemies did not prevail against our nation, and the tyrant was punished and our land purified, since they became, as it were, a ransom for the sin of our nation. Through the blood of these righteous ones and through the propitiation of their

100

death the divine providence rescued Israel, which had been shamefully treated" (17:20–22, H. Anderson, trans.). The description in 4 Maccabees 1:11 of the way Eleazar, the mother, and her seven sons died indicates that death did not vanquish them: "Not only was all humanity stirred to wonder by their courage and fortitude, but even their own torturers, and so they became responsible for the downfall of the tyranny which beset our nation, overcoming the tyrant by their fortitude so that through them their own land was purified."

This "noble" death motif repeats itself through the rest of John's Gospel, particularly in that Jesus voluntarily gives up his life only when the hour has come. His death is for the life of others, his sheep. He is "the lamb of God, who takes away the sin of the world" (1:29). Finally, Jesus is not vanquished by death, for his moment of being lifted up is the moment when he draws all to himself (12:32). John's Gospel will devote two chapters to the appearances of the risen Lord Jesus, conqueror of death. The noble death motif repeats itself also in that at Jesus' time crucifixion was the most disgraceful and shameful way to die. It was inflicted upon a person who was shamed by being nailed on a cross naked in a society that loathed nakedness. Such a death had value for no one except perhaps the government who rid itself of one more troublemaker. The crucified person was vanquished by death. But the death of Jesus, the noble shepherd who willingly lays down his life for his sheep, reverses this perception.

Jesus also shepherds other sheep: "I have other sheep that do not belong to this fold. These also I must lead, and they will hear my voice, and there will be one flock, one shepherd" (10:16). These are the Gentiles, "born not by natural generation nor by human choice nor by a man's decision but of God" (1:13). Recall the irony of John 7:35: "Surely he is not going to the dispersion among the Greeks to teach the Greeks, is he?" These are the ones that Jesus will draw to himself once he has been lifted up on the cross (12:32). These are among the 153 large fish that the disciples catch (21:11).

The imagery of gate and shepherd should not over-shadow the intimacy between Jesus and his own: "[H]e calls his own sheep by name" (10:3); "I know mine and mine know me, just as the Father knows me and I know the Father" (10:14–15); "a good [noble] shepherd lays down his life for the sheep" (10:11). This intimacy is expressed in the story of Mary of Magdala and the risen Jesus. In John 20:16 Jesus lovingly calls out the name of this sheep, "Mary." Mary responds, "Rabbouni" (teacher).

John 10:22–42: Jesus Is the Consecrated Altar of Sacrifice

22 The feast of the Dedication was then taking place in Jerusalem. It was winter. 23 And Jesus walked about in the temple area on the Portico of Solomon. 24 So the Jews gathered around him and said to him, "How long are you going to keep us in suspense? If you are the Messiah, tell us plainly." 25 Jesus answered them, "I told you and you do not believe. The works I do in my Father's name testify to me. 26 But you do not believe, because you are not among my sheep. 27 My sheep hear my voice; I know them, and they follow me. 28 I give them eternal life, and they shall never perish. No one can take them

out of my hand. ²⁹ My Father, who has given them to me, is greater than all, and no one can take them out of the Father's hand. ³⁰ The Father and I are one."

³¹ The Jews again picked up rocks to stone him. ³² Jesus answered them, "I have shown you many good works from my Father. For which of these are you trying to stone me?" ³³ The Jews answered him, "We are not stoning you for a good work but for blasphemy. You, a man, are making yourself God." ³⁴ Jesus answered them, "Is it not written in your law, 'I said, "You are gods" '? ³⁵ If it calls them gods to whom the word of God came, and scripture cannot be set aside, ³⁶ can you say that the one whom the Father has consecrated and sent into the world blasphemes because I said, 'I am the Son of God'? ³⁷ If I do not perform my Father's works, do not believe me; ³⁸ but if I perform them, even if you do not believe me, believe the works, so that you may realize [and understand] that the Father is in me and I am in the Father." ³⁹ [Then] they tried again to arrest him; but he escaped from their power.

⁴⁰ He went back across the Jordan to the place where John first baptized, and there he remained. ⁴¹ Many came to him and said, "John performed no sign, but everything John said about this man was true." ⁴² And many there began to believe in him.

The scene changes to the Portico of Solomon, the time to winter, the Feast from Tabernacles to Dedication, but Jesus is still in Jerusalem. In 165 BC the Maccabees rededicated the Temple altar that had been desecrated by Antiochus Epiphanes IV. The quotations from 2 and 4 Maccabees cited in the previous section portray the courageous and noble efforts of Eleazar as well as those of the mother and her seven sons to remain faithful to the law and God of Israel. Passages in 4 Maccabees, 1:11 and 17:20, even talk about how their land, polluted by

Antiochus' actions, was purified by their deaths. These texts foreshadow John 10:36: The Father has consecrated Jesus and sent him into the world. Jesus is the altar dedicated to God.

Verses 22–39 of this passage depict what the Synoptics present as Jesus' trial before the Sanhedrin during his last hours in Jerusalem. For example, in Luke 22:66–71, during his trial Jesus is asked the same questions as in this passage. Luke 22:67 states: "They said, 'If you are the Messiah, tell us.' " Luke 22:70 reads: "They all asked, 'Are you then the Son of God?' " In typical fashion, John uses his own language to deepen what he may have inherited from the Synoptics. In verses 22–30 Jesus interprets the question of whether he is the Messiah by referring to the works that he does in his Father's name. He also interprets the term Messiah by referring to his care for his sheep. Jesus and his Father have the same purpose and goal: to give the sheep eternal life and to prevent anyone from snatching the sheep from their folds. Thus, Messiah is an inadequate title for Jesus, the shepherd who gives his sheep eternal life, who performs his Father's works.

Verses 31–39 reinterpret the meaning of Jesus as Son of God. Jesus is not just one Jew among many who is loved by God and therefore God's son. Again Jesus refers his questioners to the works he has done, which are the works of his Father. Look at the superabundant wine at the wedding Feast of Cana. Look at Jesus' cure at a distance of a child near death. Recall Jesus' cure of the man who had been lame for thirty-eight years. Remember his feeding of five thousand people with such bounty that twelve baskets were left over. Don't forget, too, that he gave sight to a man born blind. These signs of Jesus reveal the Father at work. In the Synoptics, the verdict of Jesus' trial before the Sanhedrin is a death sentence. In John's version of this trial Jesus' conviction lies in the future; at this time the religious authorities cannot stone (31) or arrest him (39). The shepherd lays down his life for his sheep on his own terms, at his own hour.

In verses 40–42 Jesus moves away from mortal danger in Jerusalem, into Galilee. This passage also mentions for the last time the genuineness of the testimony of John the Witness: "[E]verything John said about this man was true" (41). The stage is set for Jesus' greatest sign, raising Lazarus from the dead.

These events during the Feast of Dedication invite us to reflect upon Jesus' dedication to and consecration by God, but another aspect of the Feast also merits consideration. The Maccabees delivered Israel from the rule of a tyrant who wanted to snatch them away from their God. In Jesus, who gives eternal life to his sheep, believers have a powerful and noble shepherd. No one can snatch Jesus' sheep from his grasp; no one can snatch them from the hand of his Father.

V

Fourth and Final Journey to Jerusalem via Bethany (11:1–17:26)

*John 11:1–57: Jesus Revives Lazarus
Because of Martha's and Mary's Faith*

[1] Now a man was ill, Lazarus from Bethany, the village of Mary and her sister Martha. [2] Mary was the one who had anointed the Lord with perfumed oil and dried his feet with her hair; it was her brother Lazarus who was ill. [3] So the sisters sent word to him, saying, "Master, the one you love is ill." [4] When Jesus heard this he said, "This illness is not to end in death, but is for the glory of God, that the Son of God may be glorified through it." [5] Now Jesus loved Martha and her sister and Lazarus. [6] So when he heard that he was ill, he remained for two days in the place where he was. [7] Then after this he said to his disciples, "Let us go back to Judea." [8] The disciples said to him, "Rabbi, the Jews were just trying to stone you, and you want to go back there?" [9] Jesus answered, "Are there not twelve hours in a day? If one walks during the day, he does not stumble, because he sees the light of this world. [10] But if one walks at night, he stumbles, because the light is not in him." [11] He said this, and then told them, "Our friend Lazarus is asleep, but I am going to awaken him." [12] So the disciples said to him, "Master, if he is asleep, he will be saved." [13] But Jesus was talking about his death, while they thought that he meant ordinary sleep. [14] So then Jesus said to them clearly, "Lazarus has died. [15] And I am glad for you that I was not there, that you may believe. Let us go to him." [16] So Thomas, called Didymus,

said to his fellow disciples, "Let us also go to die with him."

17 When Jesus arrived, he found that Lazarus had already been in the tomb for four days. 18 Now Bethany was near Jerusalem, only about two miles away. 19 And many of the Jews had come to Martha and Mary to comfort them about their brother. 20 When Martha heard that Jesus was coming, she went to meet him; but Mary sat at home. 21 Martha said to Jesus, "Lord, if you had been here, my brother would not have died. 22 [But] even now I know that whatever you ask of God, God will give you." 23 Jesus said to her, "Your brother will rise." 24 Martha said to him, "I know he will rise, in the resurrection on the last day." 25 Jesus told her, "I am the resurrection and the life; whoever believes in me, even if he dies, will live, 26 and everyone who lives and believes in me will never die. Do you believe this?" 27 She said to him, "Yes, Lord. I have come to believe that you are the Messiah, the Son of God, the one who is coming into the world."

28 When she had said this, she went and called her sister Mary secretly, saying, "The teacher is here and is asking for you." 29 As soon as she heard this, she rose quickly and went to him. 30 For Jesus had not yet come into the village, but was still where Martha had met him. 31 So when the Jews who were with her in the house comforting her saw Mary get up quickly and go out, they followed her, presuming that she was going to the tomb to weep there. 32 When Mary came to where Jesus was and saw him, she fell at his feet and said to him, "Lord, if you had been here, my brother would not have died." 33 When Jesus saw her weeping and the Jews who had come with her weeping, he became perturbed and deeply troubled, 34 and said, "Where have you laid him?" They said to him, "Sir, come and see." 35 And Jesus wept. 36 So the Jews said, "See how he loved him." 37 But some of them said, "Could not the one who opened the eyes of

107

the blind man have done something so that this man would not have died?"

³⁸ So Jesus, perturbed again, came to the tomb. It was a cave, and a stone lay across it. ³⁹ Jesus said, "Take away the stone." Martha, the dead man's sister, said to him, "Lord, by now there will be a stench; he has been dead for four days." ⁴⁰ Jesus said to her, "Did I not tell you that if you believe you will see the glory of God?" ⁴¹ So they took away the stone. And Jesus raised his eyes and said, "Father, I thank you for hearing me. ⁴² I know that you always hear me; but because of the crowd here I have said this, that they may believe that you sent me." ⁴³ And when he had said this, he cried out in a loud voice, "Lazarus, come out!" ⁴⁴ The dead man came out, tied hand and foot with burial bands, and his face was wrapped in a cloth. So Jesus said to them, "Untie him and let him go."

⁴⁵ Now many of the Jews who had come to Mary and seen what he had done began to believe in him. ⁴⁶ But some of them went to the Pharisees and told them what Jesus had done. ⁴⁷ So the chief priests and the Pharisees convened the Sanhedrin and said, "What are we going to do? This man is performing many signs. ⁴⁸ If we leave him alone, all will believe in him, and the Romans will come and take away both our land and our nation." ⁴⁹ But one of them, Caiaphas, who was high priest that year, said to them, "You know nothing, ⁵⁰ nor do you consider that it is better for you that one man should die instead of the people, so that the whole nation may not perish." ⁵¹ He did not say this on his own, but since he was high priest for that year, he prophesied that Jesus was going to die for the nation, ⁵² and not only for the nation, but also to gather into one the dispersed children of God. ⁵³ So from that day on they planned to kill him.

⁵⁴So Jesus no longer walked about in public among the Jews, but he left for the region near the desert, to a town called Ephraim, and there he remained with his disciples.

⁵⁵ Now the Passover of the Jews was near, and many went up from the country to Jerusalem before Passover to purify themselves. ⁵⁶ They looked for Jesus and said to one another as they were in the temple area, "What do you think? That he will not come to the feast?" ⁵⁷ For the chief priests and the Pharisees had given orders that if anyone knew where he was, he should inform them, so that they might arrest him.

In the Synoptic accounts, Jesus' cleansing of the Temple leads to his death. For example, Mark states: "The chief priests and the scribes came to hear of it and were seeking a way to put him to death" (11:18). According to John, however, the Sanhedrin plans to kill Jesus because of the miracle of giving new life to Lazarus. This is another of the many ironies in the Gospel of John: Jesus' gift of life leads to his own death, which then leads to life for his nation and for the dispersed children of God (52). In John's account, this event prompts the religious authorities to take the action first mentioned after the cure at Bethesda of the man who had been sick for thirty-eight years: "For this reason the Jews tried all the more to kill him, because he not only broke the sabbath but he also called God his own father, making himself equal to God" (5:18). Now they finally will put Jesus to death.

In biblical symbolism, seven is a perfect number. This, Jesus' seventh sign, is his greatest. In the Synoptic accounts, Jesus raised Jairus' twelve-year-old daughter (Mark 5:21–24, 35–43) and the only son of the widow of Nain (Luke 7:11–17). But this sign is his greatest because Lazarus is definitely dead. According to Jewish belief, the soul leaves the body after three days; moreover, Lazarus' corpse is giving off a stench. Just as no one had ever heard of giving sight to a man born blind, no one ever raised a person who had been dead for four days! As with the signs of the multiplication of the loaves and the healing of the beggar born blind, interpretive dialogue follows the raising of Lazarus. Through this dialogue the Evangelist presents three representative characters: Thomas, Martha, and Mary.

The opening section of this passage, verses 1–16, needs to be read carefully. Jesus performs his signs according to his own plan. He changes water into wine, heals the royal official's son, and goes up to the Feast of Tabernacles not when others ask him, but when he chooses to do so. He does not allow himself to be pushed. While all seven signs in this Gospel depict Jesus' divine nature, this story also highlights his human side. As verse 5 states, Jesus "... loved Martha and her sister and Lazarus," and verse 35 describes him weeping at the tomb. The Evangelist does not explain the source of Jesus' love for this family, but in 15:15 he does hint that it goes beyond mere human love: "I have called you friends, because I have told you everything I have heard from my Father."

Also worth scrutiny is Thomas and his striking statement, "Let us also go to die with him" (16). John does not mention Thomas in the list of disciples who were first recruited (1:35–51), but does include him here. Like Nicodemus, his first appearance is followed by others. In 14:5 Thomas displays his ignorance when he says "Master, we do not know where you are going; how can we know the way?" so Jesus must teach him. In 20:24–29 he declines to believe that the risen Jesus has appeared to the disciples, but later confesses, "My Lord and my God," addressing Jesus with the titles that Emperor Domitian claimed for himself. Thomas appears for the last time when he goes fishing and enjoys the Feast of reconciliation that the risen Jesus provides for his disciples (21:2–13). Perhaps Thomas represents Christians whose faith may ebb and flow, but who do not waver.

Feminist scholars cite Martha as a representative figure and note the prominence that women may have had in the Johannine community. In this Gospel neither Peter nor the Beloved Disciple professes faith as deeply as does Martha: "Yes, Lord, I have come to believe that you are the Messiah, the Son of God, the one who is coming into the world" (27). John wrote his Gospel "that you [his readers] may [come to] believe that Jesus is the Messiah, the Son of God, and that through this belief you may have life in his name" (20:31), and here he illustrates that belief through the character of Martha. Some interpreters see weakness in Martha's faith because she seems to doubt Jesus when he asks that Lazarus' tomb be opened: "Lord, by now there will be a stench; he has been dead for four days" (39), a doubt he then corrects. Some 750 years ago St. Bonaventure, never known to be a feminist, interpreted Martha's statement as demonstrating not negative doubt, but positive sympathy. He reasoned that she had mistakenly thought that the Lord wanted to see Lazarus out of compassion, and did not realize that he was about to reveal his power by raising Lazarus up. When she hears Jesus' response, she realizes that he wanted the tomb opened not to view a dead body, but to revive a dead person. Bonaventure goes on in his interpretation of this seventh sign to maintain that it was by merit of the sisters' faith that Lazarus was resuscitated.

Martha's confession of faith in Jesus is one great component of the high Christology of this narrative. Another is Jesus' reply to Martha: "I am the resurrection and the life; whoever believes in me, even if he dies, will live, and everyone who lives and believes in me will never die" (25–26). The question that ends this self-description is addressed not only to Martha, but to all readers: "Do you believe this?" Jesus' declaration of his self-identity harkens back to 5:21: "For just as the Father raises the dead and gives life, so also does the Son give life to whomever he wishes." Jesus' call to Lazarus to come forth from the tomb (43) echoes 5:28–29: "...[T]he hour is coming in which all who are in the tombs will hear his [the Son of Man's] voice and will come out." Jesus does not petition his Father for the power to raise Lazarus, for as the Father's representative he already has it (41–42). Others must assist the resuscitated Lazarus out of his burial clothes, but the risen Lord Jesus removes and carefully folds up his own (20:4–9).

The story of the raising of Lazarus concludes with responses to Jesus' greatest sign. Some begin to believe in him (45). The religious authorities, especially Caiaphas, respond by plotting Jesus' death. In yet another example of Johannine irony, the high priest thinks it is true that Jesus must be put to death to save the nation, but for believers Caiaphas' prophecy is true on a deeper level. The death of Jesus, the noble shepherd, will bring about salvation for the nation, for the Jews scattered abroad, and also for the Gentiles.

This passage contains three representative figures: Thomas, Mary, and Martha. Thomas has been discussed above, and Mary figures prominently in the next passage to be discussed, her anointing of Jesus' feet (12:1–8). Martha, who professed her faith in Jesus, is indeed a strong figure. She and Jesus are friends. In verse 4 Jesus told his disciples that what he will do " … is for the glory of God, that the Son of God may be glorified through it." He did not tell them, or Martha, that it is their belief that will allow them to see that glory. To her, however, he speaks plainly: "Did I not tell you that if you believe you will see the glory of God?" (40). Contemporary believers also can see this seventh sign as a reflection of the glory of God who can give life to the dead, and they also can learn from Martha, the representative character, as they profess the same profound faith in Jesus that she has.

John 12:1–8: Mary's Generous Act Anticipates Jesus' Washing His Disciples' Feet

[1] Six days before Passover Jesus came to Bethany, where Lazarus was, whom Jesus had raised from the dead. [2] They gave a dinner for him there, and Martha served, while Lazarus was one of those reclining at table with him. [3] Mary took a liter of costly perfumed oil made from genuine aromatic nard and anointed the feet of Jesus and dried them with her hair; the house was filled with the fragrance of the oil. [4] Then Judas the Iscariot, one [of] his disciples, and the one who would betray him, said, [5] "Why was this oil not sold for three hundred days' wages and given to the poor?" [6] He said this not because he cared about the poor but because he was a thief and held the money bag and used to steal the contributions. [7] So Jesus said, "Leave her alone. Let her keep this for the day of my burial. [8] You always have the poor with you, but you do not always have me."

Overfamiliarity with this precious story or separating it from its context saps its originality and power. It calls for a careful, fresh reading.

During the raising of Lazarus (11:1–44) Martha occupied a central role, but this story revolves around her sister, Mary. While John does not state directly that Jesus' disciples were present, Judas' remark suggests that they were. More importantly, reclining at table was Lazarus, the friend Jesus had raised from the dead, perhaps enjoying a feast in honor of his new life. The family of Martha, Mary, and Lazarus seems wealthy in that they could afford a full liter of precious perfume, the value of which Judas sets at 300 days' wages — for a contemporary minimum-wage worker, almost $24,000! Usually, nard would be used on the head, but Mary anoints Jesus' feet. Finally, only the Gospel of John notes that " … the house was filled with the fragrance of the oil" (3), perhaps a counterpoint to the observation in the previous episode that Lazarus would surely fill the entire air with a horrid stench (11:39).

Many commentaries divide John's Gospel into The Book of Signs (1–12) and The Book of Glory (13–21). Such a division diminishes many of the connections between what precedes this story in chapter 11 and what follows in chapters 13–21. Since the Sanhedrin had already planned to kill Jesus, he was under the threat of death; the phrase "six days before Passover" suggests that it indeed is nigh, for he was executed during Passover. In this context, Mary's anointing can be seen as a preparation for his imminent burial. Most importantly, Mary's anointing of Jesus' feet anticipates Jesus' washing his own disciples' feet during the Last Supper. Perhaps Mary's action suggested to Jesus his gesture of generous love.

This passage contrasts two representative characters, one positive and one negative. Mary is exalted because of her generosity; Judas is denounced for his greed. These characters and their actions challenge all Christian congregations to examine not only how they allocate their financial resources, but their motives for doing so.

John 12:9–19: The Crowd Hails Jesus as King Because He Had Raised Lazarus

9 [The] large crowd of the Jews found out that he was there and came, not only because of Jesus, but also to see Lazarus, whom he had raised from the dead. 10 And the chief priests plotted to kill Lazarus too, 11 because many of the Jews were turning away and believing in Jesus because of him.

12 On the next day, when the great crowd that had come to the feast heard that Jesus was coming to Jerusalem, 13 they took palm branches and went out to meet him, and cried out: "Hosanna!/ Blessed is he who comes in the name of the Lord,/ [even] the king of Israel."

14 Jesus found an ass and sat upon it, as is written: 15 "Fear no more, O daughter Zion;/ see, your king comes, seated upon an ass's colt." 16 His disciples did not understand this at first, but when Jesus had been glorified they remembered that these things were written about him and that they had done this for him. 17 So the crowd that was with him when he called Lazarus from the tomb and raised him from death continued to testify. 18 This was [also] why the crowd went to meet him, because they heard that he had done this sign. 19 So the Pharisees said to one another, "You see that you are gaining nothing. Look, the whole world has gone after him."

This passage differs markedly from accounts in the Synoptic Gospels. Only John's Gospel mentions the palm branches, which since the time of the Maccabees had been a sign of national liberation. Events in this passage resemble the description of the Feast of Dedication in 2 Maccabees: "Carrying rods entwined with leaves, green branches and palms, they sang hymns of grateful praise to him who had brought about the purification of his own Place" (10:7). In John's Gospel, Jesus himself, not his disciples, fetches the donkey on which he rides into Jerusalem. Moreover, in John the crowd comes to Jesus because of his seventh and greatest sign, the raising of Lazarus. This passage begins and ends with references to Lazarus. Jesus will go to his death for raising his friend from the dead and will attract the whole world to himself. Ironically, the Pharisees say, "Look, the whole world has gone after him" (19). John alone contains the reflection, "His disciples did not understand this at first, but when Jesus had been glorified they remembered that these things were written about him and that they had done this for him" (16), which informs readers that the Scriptures and events in Jesus' life interpret one another.

Verses 13–15 contain references which, as verse 16 hints, are not found at any other place in Scripture. Deep reflection and the Paraclete guided the Johannine community in discovering links between Jesus' entry into Jerusalem and Psalm 118: "Blessed is he/ who comes in the name of the LORD" (26); Zephaniah 3: "The king of Israel" (15); Zephaniah 3: "Fear not, O Zion" (16); Zechariah 9: "Rejoice heartily, O daughter Zion/... See, your king shall come to you;/ a just savior is he,/ Meek, and riding on an ass ..." (9). One theme connects these references: God coming as king, in a humble manner, for the salvation of his people. Jesus does not enter Jerusalem riding in a war chariot, but on a beast of burden. Ever since Nathanael called Jesus "King of Israel" (1:49), this gospel has been inviting readers to figure out how Jesus is king. Jesus ran away when he saw that the crowds wanted to make him king because he had the power to supply physical food (6:14–15). In this passage Jesus, who had shown his divine power in raising Lazarus, arrives in the city of his death in a most humble manner. John will return to this theme when Jesus confronts Pilate (18:33–38).

The disciples are nowhere to be seen. This is Jesus' hour. As the noble shepherd, he lays down his life and takes it up again, as Paul states in his letter to the Philippians: " … [T]hough he was in the form of God,/ [he] did not regard equality with God something to be grasped./ Rather, …/ he humbled himself … " (2:6–8). Contemporary Christians, clerics and lay alike, may well ask themselves how they wear their authority.

John 12:20–36a: The Significance of Jesus' Being Lifted Up From the Earth for Gentiles

20 Now there were some Greeks among those who had come up to worship at the feast. 21 They came to Philip, who was from Bethsaida in Galilee, and asked him, "Sir, we would like to see Jesus." 22 Philip went and told Andrew; then Andrew and Philip went and told Jesus. 23 Jesus answered them, "The hour has come for the Son of Man to be glorified. 24 Amen, amen, I say to you, unless a grain of wheat falls to the ground and dies, it remains just a grain of wheat; but if it dies, it produces much fruit. 25 Whoever loves his life loses it, and whoever hates his

life in this world will preserve it for eternal life. ²⁶ Whoever serves me must follow me, and where I am, there also will my servant be. The Father will honor whoever serves me.

²⁷ "I am troubled now. Yet what should I say? 'Father, save me from this hour'? But it was for this purpose that I came to this hour. ²⁸ Father, glorify your name." Then a voice came from heaven, "I have glorified it and will glorify it again." ²⁹ The crowd there heard it and said it was thunder; but others said, "An angel has spoken to him." ³⁰ Jesus answered and said, "This voice did not come for my sake but for yours. ³¹ Now is the time of judgment on this world; now the ruler of this world will be driven out. ³² And when I am lifted up from the earth, I will draw everyone to myself." ³³ He said this indicating the kind of death he would die. ³⁴ So the crowd answered him, "We have heard from the law that the Messiah remains forever. Then how can you say that the Son of Man must be lifted up? Who is this Son of Man?" ³⁵ Jesus said to them, "The light will be among you only a little while. Walk while you have the light, so that darkness may not overcome you. Whoever walks in the dark does not know where he is going. ³⁶ While you have the light, believe in the light, so that you may become children of the light."

Although his passage has no clear narrative structure, it does present the key idea of Jesus' mission to the Gentiles. In 12:19 John presented the ironic truth that the whole world has gone after Jesus. Now verses 20–22 tell how the Gentile proselytes or God-fearers want to see Jesus. Although the passage never really says whether these Gentiles got to see Jesus, the verses that follow indicate how Jesus will win over these non-Jews. He will give his life as the grain of wheat that dies, so that it may produce much fruit (24). Jesus' hour has finally come, and he will glorify his Father not only through his signs, but also through his death (27–30), a death that destroys the barriers that separate all from God (31). Perhaps the most important verse is this one: "And when I am lifted up from the earth, I will draw everyone to myself" (32). Twice before John has hinted at this prediction ("And just as Moses lifted up the serpent in the desert, so must the Son of Man be lifted up.... " [3:14]; "When you lift up the Son of Man, then you will realize that I AM.... " [8:28]). Now, however, the Evangelist specifies that through his crucifixion Jesus will draw all people to himself.

John frequently uses the image of light. The Word is light (1:4–5, 9). Jesus is the light of the world (8:12) and gives the light of sight, physical and spiritual, to the man born blind. John also contrasts light and darkness as images of ethical conduct, as he does in 3:19–20: "And this is the verdict, that the light came into the world, but people preferred darkness to light, because their works were evil. For everyone who does wicked things hates the light and does not come toward the light, so that his works might not be exposed." The Evangelist concludes this section with light imagery. Jesus is the light, and now people must realize that his light shines beyond the boundaries of the elect to the non-elect Gentiles. Believers in Jesus and his universal mission "become children of the light."

John 12:36b–50: Dual Summary of Jesus' Ministry of Signs and Word

36bAfter he had said this, Jesus left and hid from them. 37 Although he had performed so many signs in their presence they did not believe in him, 38 in order that the word which Isaiah the prophet spoke might be fulfilled: "Lord, who has believed our preaching,/ to whom has the might of the Lord been revealed?" [39] For this reason they could not believe, because again Isaiah said: [40] "He blinded their eyes/ and hardened their heart,/ so that they might not see with their eyes/ and understand with their heart and be converted,/ and I would heal them." [41] Isaiah said this because he saw his glory and spoke about him. [42] Nevertheless, many, even among the authorities, believed in him, but because of the Pharisees they did not acknowledge it openly in order not to be expelled from the synagogue. [43] For they preferred human praise to the glory of God.

[44] Jesus cried out and said, "Whoever believes in me believes not only in me but also in the one who sent me, [45] and whoever sees me sees the one who sent me. [46] I came into the world as light, so that everyone who believes in me might not remain in darkness. [47] And if anyone hears my words and does not observe them, I do not condemn him, for I did not come to condemn the world but to save the world. [48] Whoever rejects me and does not accept my words has something to judge him: the word that I spoke, it will condemn him on the last day, [49] because I did not speak on my own, but the Father who sent me commanded me what to say and speak. [50] And I know that his commandment is eternal life. So what I say, I say as the Father told me."

This passage, which falls into two parts (12:36b–43 and 12:44–50), mentions no clear place, time, and audience. For example, since Jesus is in hiding, to whom does he cry out? "The Jews"? His disciples? The context suggests that the Evangelist is addressing his readers.

Concerning the first part, John's Gospel presents seven marvelous signs and mentions in passing others that Jesus performed, as in 2:23; 3:2; 6:2, 26; 7:36; 10:32; and

11:47. The first chapters are bound together by these signs. Through them, Jesus revealed his Father's glory and God's redemptive will for every person. But the Prologue had already signaled the mystery that Jesus would not receive a great welcome among his own (1:11).

Like other New Testament authors, the Evangelist tries to explain this largely negative reaction to Jesus' signs among "the Jews." It was the same reaction that their ancestors gave to Isaiah: "Who would believe what we have heard?" (53:1). Reflecting a worldview that did not understand the notion of secondary causality, Isaiah attributes this negative response to God himself: "[H]e [God, speaking to Isaiah] replied: Go and say to this people: Listen carefully, but you shall not understand!/ Look intently, but you shall know nothing!/ You are to make the heart of this people sluggish,/ to dull their ears and close their eyes;/ Else their eyes will see, their ears hear,/ their heart understand,/ and they will turn and be healed" (6:9–10).

Some, even from among the religious authorities, believed in Jesus but dared not acknowledge him for fear of being expelled from the synagogue. It is easy to condemn such people, but being thrown out of the synagogue was a type of death sentence. They would have severed their ties to a close-knit neighborhood and all its social, economic, and cultural connections. Professing belief in Jesus would have cast them overboard into a turbulent sea without a life preserver.

The second part of this passage presents yet another appeal to the readers of this Gospel. Do you believe that Jesus is the one sent from the Father? Are you really listening to Jesus' words and following them? Are you walking in Jesus' light or in darkness? Andrew T. Lincoln and others have depicted John's Gospel as a cosmic trial. From the very first chapter the religious authorities have sought to prosecute Jesus, whose words and signs have borne witness to him as the one sent from God. In reality, it is Jesus who has put his opponents on trial. This phase of the courtroom drama concludes with a stark judgment: "Whoever rejects me and does not accept my words has something to judge him: the word that I spoke, it will condemn him on the last day" (48). The consequences of the Johannine cosmic trial are not limited to the audience to whom the historical Jesus may have been speaking. Decades ago the pre-eminent German commentator on John, Rudolf Bultmann, presented a most challenging point: what is played out on a cosmic canvas is also played out in each individual's heart.

John 13:1–30: In Jesus' Community the World's Standards Are Turned Upside Down

¹ Before the feast of Passover, Jesus knew that his hour had come to pass from this world to the Father. He loved his own in the world and he loved them to the end. ² The devil had already induced Judas, son of Simon the Iscariot, to hand him over. So, during supper, ³ fully aware that the Father had put everything into his power and that he had come from God and was returning to God, ⁴ he rose from supper and took off his outer garments. He took a towel and tied it around his waist. ⁵ Then he poured water into a basin and began to wash the disciples' feet and dry them with the towel around his waist. ⁶ He came to Simon Peter, who said to him, "Master, are you going to wash my feet?" ⁷ Jesus answered and said to

him, "What I am doing, you do not understand now, but you will understand later." ⁸ Peter said to him, "You will never wash my feet." Jesus answered him, "Unless I wash you, you will have no inheritance with me." ⁹ Simon Peter said to him, "Master, then not only my feet, but my hands and head as well." ¹⁰ Jesus said to him, "Whoever has bathed has no need except to have his feet washed, for he is clean all over; so you are clean, but not all." ¹¹ For he knew who would betray him; for this reason, he said, "Not all of you are clean."

¹² So when he had washed their feet [and] put his garments back on and reclined at table again, he said to them, "Do you realize what I have done for you? ¹³ You call me 'teacher' and 'master,' and rightly so, for indeed I am. ¹⁴ If I, therefore, the master and teacher, have washed your feet, you ought to wash one another's feet. ¹⁵ I have given you a model to follow, so that as I have done for you, you should also do. ¹⁶ Amen, amen, I say to you, no slave is greater than his master nor any messenger greater than the one who sent him. ¹⁷ If you understand this, blessed are you if you do it. ¹⁸ I am not speaking of all of you. I know those whom I have chosen. But so that the scripture might be fulfilled, 'The one who ate my food has raised his heel against me.' ¹⁹ From now on I am telling you before it happens, so that when it happens you may believe that I AM. ²⁰ Amen, amen, I say to you, whoever receives the one I send receives me, and whoever receives me receives the one who sent me."

²¹ When he had said this, Jesus was deeply troubled and testified, "Amen, amen, I say to you, one of you will betray me." ²² The disciples looked at one another, at a loss as to whom he meant. ²³ One of his disciples, the one whom Jesus loved, was reclining at Jesus' side. ²⁴ So Simon Peter nodded to him to find out whom he meant. ²⁵ He leaned back against Jesus' chest and said to him,

"Master, who is it?" [26] Jesus answered, "It is the one to whom I hand the morsel after I have dipped it." So he dipped the morsel and [took it and] handed it to Judas, son of Simon the Iscariot. [27] After he took the morsel, Satan entered him. So Jesus said to him, "What you are going to do, do quickly." [28] [Now] none of those reclining at table realized why he said this to him. [29] Some thought that since Judas kept the money bag, Jesus had told him, "Buy what we need for the feast," or to give something to the poor.[30] So he took the morsel and left at once. And it was night.

In this passage John describes Jesus' last supper with his disciples, but what he recounts is neither a Passover meal nor is it the first Eucharist. In 6:51–58, the passage in which Jesus describes himself as "the living bread that came down from heaven," the Evangelist indicated clearly that his community celebrates the Eucharist, but he never narrates a specific event in which it was instituted. The Johannine word for Jesus' intimate followers is "disciple," not "twelve apostles," so this account leaves open the number and gender of "the disciples" whose feet Jesus washes. A symposium meal is depicted, where the participants reclined with their feet at the outer edge of the couches. Thus it was easy for Jesus to walk behind his disciples and wash their feet. Also it seems that the Beloved Disciple and Judas have positions of honor near him, so that the Beloved Disciple can lean on his bosom and Jesus can easily hand Judas a choice morsel. "The Beloved Disciple" who first appears here will be depicted subsequently (see John 18:15; 19:25–27; 20:2–10; 21:7; 21:20–23) as more beloved and loyal than Peter. It is widely assumed that the witness of this Beloved Disciple stands behind the

Fourth Gospel. At this point of the narrative the combative "Jews" are no longer mentioned. Jesus commences teaching his disciples alone. In the lines that follow this passage (13:31–14:31) his teaching takes the form of an eloquent farewell discourse. Finally, the Evangelist's method of contrasting the representative characters of the Beloved Disciple and Peter and Judas deserves careful attention. If we do not let John be John, we will miss the true import of this passage.

To wash another person's feet was a most degrading task. Ordinary people did not wear shoes. Houses did not have toilets. Human and animal waste filled the streets and footpaths, and people prayed for rain to cleanse them of this foul refuse. Washing your own feet was noisome enough; it was a slave's work to wash another's. With great frequency and clarity this Gospel has shown, especially through Jesus' signs, that he is the one sent by God, God's Son. Out of complete love for his disciples he is performing the demeaning task of washing their feet. Other passages in John's Gospel (the miracle at Cana, Jesus' feeding the five thousand, Thomas addressing him as "My Lord and my God") have put Jesus at the same level as the Roman Emperor. It is unimaginable that an emperor would do anything like this. But Jesus doesn't wash his disciples' feet merely to demonstrate how, by serving and loving one another, they should resist imperial standards. By washing their feet he is pointing to his death on the cross. How? Jesus takes off and puts on his clothing (4, 12). In naming this action, the Evangelist uses the same Greek words that he employs to depict the noble shepherd's laying down and taking up his life (10:17–18). If Peter doesn't allow Jesus to wash his feet, he no longer is walking with Jesus. That is, if Peter doesn't take on himself the effects of Jesus' death and glorification, then he no longer can count himself among Jesus' disciples. Verse 10, "Whoever has bathed has no need except to have his feet washed, for he is clean all over; so you are clean, but not all," is difficult to interpret, but "to bathe" is best explained by the parallel statement in 15:3: "You are already pruned because of the word that I spoke to you." While Jesus' word cleanses and bathes, it is Jesus' death and glorification on the cross, symbolized in his washing of his disciples' feet, which makes them truly clean. The church celebrates Jesus' request, "Do this in memory of me" (Lk 22:19), in the breaking of the bread every time the Eucharist is celebrated, but finds a place for celebrating this other powerful symbol that celebrates Jesus' actions at the Last Supper only once a year, on Holy Thursday. The fact that it is memorialized so infrequently does not diminish its power and importance.

Jesus has already called Satan a liar and a murderer (8:44). The "father of lies" now enters Judas (27), the keeper of the money bag, described in the previous chapter as "a thief" (12:6). Ironically, the other disciples, who do not understand what he is about, think he is going to help the poor. Jesus has displayed his love for him by washing his feet and giving him a choice morsel; now Judas leaves the Last Supper and goes out into the night. The one who fulfills Psalm 41:10 ("Even the friend who had my trust,/ who shared my table, has scorned me") goes out not into ordinary darkness, but into moral darkness. Recall John 3:19: "And this is the verdict, that the light came into the world, but people preferred darkness to light, because their works were evil." Although Jesus clearly understands what Judas intends to do, it is also clear that Judas is not predetermined to betray Jesus, but does so willingly and continues to walk in darkness.

The representative characters of this passage present ordinary believers with plenty of challenges to their preconceived notions. The disciple whom Jesus loves is contrasted with greedy Judas, whose person and deed resound through this passage like a dirge. The Evangelist also contrasts the Beloved Disciple with Peter, who misunderstands what Jesus is about as he washes his feet and who has to go through the disciple whom Jesus loves to find out the betrayer's identity. Steadfast love is contrasted with backstabbing betrayal. Steadfast love is contrasted with the oafish Peter, who doesn't understand what is going on and clings desperately to his identity as a disciple. In its concluding chapter, 21, John's Gospel will describe Peter's rehabilitation.

John 13:31–14:31: Jesus Consoles and Challenges Present and Future Disciples

31 When he had left, Jesus said, "Now is the Son of Man glorified, and God is glorified in him. 32 [If God is glorified in him,] God will also glorify him in himself, and he will glorify him at once. 33 My children, I will be with you only a little while longer. You will look for me, and as I told the Jews, 'Where I go you cannot come,' so now I say it to you. 34 I give you a new commandment: love one another. As I have loved you, so you also should love one another. 35 This is how all will know that you are my disciples, if you have love for one another."

36 Simon Peter said to him, "Master, where are you going?" Jesus answered [him], "Where I am going, you

cannot follow me now, though you will follow later." [37] Peter said to him, "Master, why can't I follow you now? I will lay down my life for you." [38] Jesus answered, "Will you lay down your life for me? Amen, amen, I say to you, the cock will not crow before you deny me three times."

[14:1] "Do not let your hearts be troubled. You have faith in God; have faith also in me. [2] In my Father's house there are many dwelling places. If there were not, would I have told you that I am going to prepare a place for you? [3] And if I go and prepare a place for you, I will come back again and take you to myself, so that where I am you also may be. [4] Where [I] am going you know the way." [5] Thomas said to him, "Master, we do not know where you are going; how can we know the way?" [6] Jesus said to him, "I am the way and the truth and the life. No one comes to the Father except through me. [7] If you know me, then you will also know my Father. From now on you do know him and have seen him." [8] Philip said to him, "Master, show us the Father, and that will be enough for us." [9] Jesus said to him, "Have I been with you for so long a time and you still do not know me, Philip? Whoever has seen me has seen the Father. How can you say, 'Show us the Father'? [10] Do you not believe that I am in the Father and the Father is in me? The words that I speak to you I do not speak on my own. The Father who dwells in me is doing his works. [11] Believe me that I am in the Father and the Father is in me, or else, believe because of the works themselves. [12] Amen, amen, I say to you, whoever believes in me will do the works that I do, and will do greater ones than these, because I am going to the Father. [13] And whatever you ask in my name, I will do, so that the Father may be glorified in the Son. [14] If you ask anything of me in my name, I will do it. [15] "If you love me, you will keep my commandments. [16] And I will ask the Father, and he will give you another Advocate to be with you always, ¹⁷ the Spirit of truth, which the world cannot accept, because it neither sees nor knows it. But you know it, because it remains with you, and will be in you. ¹⁸ I will not leave you orphans; I will come to you. ¹⁹ In a little while the world will no longer see me, but you will see me, because I live and you will live. ²⁰ On that day you will realize that I am in my Father and you are in me and I in you. ²¹ Whoever has my commandments and observes them is the one who loves me. And whoever loves me will be loved by my Father, and I will love him and reveal myself to him." ²² Judas, not the Iscariot, said to him, "Master, [then] what happened that you will reveal yourself to us and not to the world?" ²³ Jesus answered and said to him, "Whoever loves me will keep my word, and my Father will love him, and we will come to him and make our dwelling with him. ²⁴ Whoever does not love me does not keep my words; yet the word you hear is not mine but that of the Father who sent me.

²⁵ "I have told you this while I am with you. ²⁶ The Advocate, the holy Spirit that the Father will send in my name — he will teach you everything and remind you of all that [I] told you. ²⁷ Peace I leave with you; my peace I give to you. Not as the world gives do I give it to you. Do not let your hearts be troubled or afraid. ²⁸ You heard me tell you, 'I am going away and I will come back to you.' If you loved me, you would rejoice that I am going to the Father; for the Father is greater than I. ²⁹ And now I have told you this before it happens, so that when it happens you may believe. ³⁰ I will no longer speak much with you, for the ruler of the world is coming. He has no power over me, ³¹ but the world must know that I love the Father and that I do just as the Father has commanded me. Get up, let us go."

Five chapters in the Gospel of John, 13 through 17, are written in the literary motif of a farewell discourse. Other examples of this motif occur in Paul's farewell address to the Ephesian elders (Acts 20:17–38) and in the form of the Second Letter to Timothy. In this motif an important figure who is about to die hands on to his children or disciples the legacy of his life and teaching and exhorts them to be steadfast in following his teaching and commandments amid various difficulties.

The Gospel of John deviates from the usual pattern of this motif in that it has Jesus speaking not only of his departure, but also of his return. The Farewell Discourse in John also differs from the usual pattern by speaking of the one who will empower the disciples to understand Jesus' teaching and to embody it amid persecution. That is the role of the Paraclete or Advocate, the Holy Spirit, who will teach the disciples everything and remind them of all that Jesus told them (14:26). Further, this Farewell Discourse imparts consolation to the disciples who are losing their Master, but the Evangelist will not allow this consolation to sink into self-pity. Rather he exhorts them to get on with being Jesus' disciples in and for the world through their works. It might seem that the Farewell Discourse is directed to the disciples present in this particular scene, but actually all who read John are the audience. John 13–17 blends perspective and time, as it has Jesus speak in the present, as though the gifts of the future are already present. Further, although the address began at Jesus' symposium or last meal with his disciples, this setting seems to float away. The symposium began with a meal then moves on to a teaching, which now becomes the sole focus. As one scholar has put it, Jesus' Farewell

Discourse is a feast of words. Reading John 13–17 is like walking up a spiral staircase; the same things keep coming into view, but from different angles.

In this section the Evangelist uses four disciples — Peter, Thomas, Philip, and Judas — to keep the action going.

As in the Synoptics, the disciple who will deny Jesus, Peter, boasts: "Master, why can't I follow you now? I will lay down my life for you" (13:37). As mentioned earlier, in 21:15–19 the Evangelist will describe Peter's rehabilitation. Once forgiven and commissioned, Peter will indeed follow Jesus.

In John 11:16, Thomas encouraged his fellow disciples: "Let us also go to die with him." In John 20:24–29 the risen Lord Jesus appears to Thomas, who eventually utters this lofty profession of faith: "My Lord and my God!" John 21:2 notes that Thomas was a fisherman. In this passage Thomas' question leads to another of Jesus' "I am" sayings: "I am the way and the truth and the life" (14:6). Jesus has come from the Father and leads the way back to the Father by revealing the truth through word and signs about God and by giving the life that comes from God. If Thomas knows Jesus and his words and signs, then he will also know the Father who has sent Jesus (14:7).

Philip is first mentioned in John's recruitment stories (1:43–45). It is Philip that Jesus asks about feeding the five thousand (6:5–7). It is to Philip that the Gentile God-fearers come when they want to see Jesus (12:21–22). Philip's request in 14:8, "Master, show us the Father, and that will be enough for us," allows Jesus to launch into a long statement that he himself, especially through his works, has already revealed the Father to the disciples.

In 14:22 Judas, not the Iscariot, mentioned for the first and only time, asks a question that allows Jesus to explain how, through the Advocate, he will reveal himself to the disciples and not to a world hostile to such revelation.

Climbing the spiral staircase of this section (14:1–14), readers see a frequently recurring theme of faith, as in verse 11: "Believe me that I am in the Father and the Father is in me, or else, believe because of the works themselves." The theme of love, introduced in 13:34–35, also runs through much of 14:15–24; for instance, "Whoever has my commandments and observes them is the one who loves me" (14:21). Further, the theme of the Advocate or Paraclete pulses through 14:15–26. The Advocate will help the disciples not only to see into the deep meaning of Jesus' teaching and signs (26), but also to help them in their witness to the world ("[T]he Spirit of truth that proceeds from the Father, he will testify to me. And you also testify" [15:26–27]) and in their lawsuit against the world ("And when he [The Advocate] comes he will convict the world in regard to sin and righteousness and condemnation ..." [16:8–11]).

For centuries 14:31 has puzzled commentators. Jesus says, "Get up, let us go," and then goes on speaking for three more chapters. Scholars have found some parallels in Greek drama for this type of delayed exit, a device still used by playwrights today. For example, at the conclusion of contemporary composer John Adams' *Dr. Atomic*, the main character, a representation of the historical figure J. Robert Oppenheimer, exits and returns several times during his final aria. It is a powerful scene, as it suggests how the character knows the action he must take, but resists moving forward into it.

Jesus' voice sounds so authoritative in his Farewell Discourse because he is speaking as the Risen Lord, who has been glorified by his death. Indeed, he has gone away from his disciples through death and has come back to them as the Risen Lord (14:28). In 14:12 he gives the community of disciples their marching orders: "Amen, amen, I say to you, whoever believes in me will do the works that I do, and will do greater works than these, because I am going to the Father." Jesus gave drink to the thirsty, fed the hungry, cured the sick, gave sight to the blind, and raised the dead. The disciples' works will be greater because their numbers will be greater and they will be performing these signs all over the world. The representative character of Peter offers us encouragement when we fail. Thomas, Philip, and the faithful Judas did not run away when Jesus' teaching demanded the greatest commitment, unlike many disciples who, after being told in the synagogue at Capernaum that they must eat his flesh and drink his blood "returned to their former way of life and no longer accompanied him" (6:66). These four have remained with him, ever eager to be enlightened in his ways.

John 15:1–17: Jesus Truly Represents God's People and Bears Fruit through Believers

¹ "I am the true vine, and my Father is the vine grower. ² He takes away every branch in me that does not bear fruit, and everyone that does he prunes so that it bears more fruit. ³ You are already pruned because of the word that I spoke to you. ⁴ Remain in me, as I remain in you. Just as a branch cannot bear fruit on its own unless it remains on the vine, so neither can you unless you

remain in me. [5] I am the vine, you are the branches. Whoever remains in me and I in him will bear much fruit, because without me you can do nothing. [6] Anyone who does not remain in me will be thrown out like a branch and wither; people will gather them and throw them into a fire and they will be burned. [7] If you remain in me and my words remain in you, ask for whatever you want and it will be done for you. [8] By this is my Father glorified, that you bear much fruit and become my disciples. [9] As the Father loves me, so I also love you. Remain in my love. [10] If you keep my commandments, you will remain in my love, just as I have kept my Father's commandments and remain in his love.

[11] "I have told you this so that my joy may be in you and your joy may be complete. [12] This is my commandment: love one another as I love you. [13] No one has greater love than this, to lay down one's life for one's friends. [14] You are my friends if you do what I command you. [15] I no longer call you slaves, because a slave does not know what his master is doing. I have called you friends, because I have told you everything I have heard from my Father. [16] It was not you who chose me, but I who chose you and appointed you to go and bear fruit that will remain, so that whatever you ask the Father in my name he may give you. [17] This I command you: love one another."

This, the best known passage in John's Farewell Discourse, has been the subject of many sacred hymns and catechetical instructions. Isaiah 5:1–7 presents an expressive Old Testament parallel: "The vineyard of the LORD of hosts is the house of Israel,/ and the people of Judah are his cherished plant;/ He looked for judgment, but see, bloodshed!/ for justice, but hark, the outcry!" (7). Indeed, God's chosen people were God's vineyard, but as this verse from Isaiah indicates, Israel often failed to bear fruit. This indictment resounds most clearly in Ezekiel 15, 17, and 19. In contrast to a vine that did not bear fruit is Jesus, God's true vine, who through those who believe in him will bear much fruit.

This passage develops the theme of love already sounded in 13:34–35 ("As I have loved you, so you also should love one another. This is how all will know that you are my disciples, if you have love for one another") and 14:21 ("[W]hoever loves me will be loved by my Father, and I will love him and reveal myself to him)". Jesus reiterates: "This is my commandment: love one another as I love you. No one has greater love than this, to lay down one's life for one's friends" (12–13). Building upon Greco-Roman notions of friendship, the Evangelist states that Jesus' disciples are better than his slaves. Indeed, they are his "friends" because he has withheld no secret from them, and has told them everything he has heard from his Father (15). Such an idea of sharing intimate knowledge resonates with the cleansing power of God's word (3). God's word in Jesus is not outside believers, but has its effect within them as they remain on the vine that is Jesus.

In the spiral staircase of John's Farewell Discourse, verses 7 and 16 provide another glimpse at the role that prayer plays for the disciples. The previous chapter had already announced this theme: "And whatever you ask in my name, I will do, so that the Father may be glorified in the Son. If you ask anything of me in my name, I will do it" (14:13–14). John 15:7 adds: "If you remain in me and my words remain in you, ask for whatever you want and it will be done for you." Verse 16 provides a variation: "[I] appointed you to go and bear fruit that will remain, so that whatever you ask the Father in my name he may give you." Verses 23–27 of the next chapter also develop this theme. Like branches on the vine the disciples pray in dependence upon Jesus, intimately and with his power. They pray to the Father through Jesus and in conformity with Jesus' commandments.

It is easy to read this passage as an expression of a comfortable "Me and Jesus" spirituality: I'm an intimate branch on Jesus, the true vine. However, this passage moves beyond such a comfy relationship with the decidedly corporate dimension of its love commandment: love another to the point of death. In tours of vineyards in the Napa Valley of California and in the Finger Lakes of New York I've been amazed to see how drastically vinedressers cut back the plants. It seems that there could never be another harvest. But lo and behold, next year they produce a bumper crop. May every reader have a spiritual experience like this one in nature: pruned, it seems, to the very ground of our being, Jesus raises us up to bear much fruit.

John 15:18–16:4a: The Disciples, Empowered by the Advocate, Take On the World

18 "If the world hates you, realize that it hated me first. 19 If you belonged to the world, the world would love its own; but because you do not belong to the world, and I have chosen you out of the world, the world hates you. 20 Remember the word I spoke to you, 'No slave is greater than his master.' If they persecuted me, they will also persecute you. If they kept my word, they will also keep yours. 21 And they will do all these things to you on account of my name, because they do not know the one who sent me. 22 If I had not come and spoken to them, they would have no sin; but as it is they have no excuse for their sin. 23 Whoever hates me also hates my Father.

[24] If I had not done works among them that no one else ever did, they would not have sin; but as it is, they have seen and hated both me and my Father. [25] But in order that the word written in their law might be fulfilled, 'They hated me without cause.'

[26] "When the Advocate comes whom I will send you from the Father, the Spirit of truth that proceeds from the Father, he will testify to me. [27] And you also testify, because you have been with me from the beginning. [16:1] "I have told you this so that you may not fall away. [2] They will expel you from the synagogues; in fact, the hour is coming when everyone who kills you will think he is offering worship to God. [3] They will do this because they have not known either the Father or me. [4a] I have told you this so that when their hour comes you may remember that I told you."

After offering the comforting words that they are branches on the true vine, Jesus, the Evangelist brings the disciples face to face with the hatred that the world will pour out on them. If the world has hated the vine, why should the branches not expect the same reproach? The spiral staircase of Jesus' Farewell Discourse in the Gospel of John contained earlier references to the world turned away from God and the one God has sent. For example, 14:19 states, "In a little while the world will no longer see me, but you will see me, because I live and you will live" (see also 14:17, 22). Now the Evangelist warns off the world's hostility. Although it was the Jews who for the most part persecuted John's community (see 16:2), the Roman powers-that-be also oppressed Christians who challenged their power, policies, and treatment of people subject to them. Consider how for relatively minor infractions Paul was arrested and imprisoned for months, and eventually executed. All across the empire, proclaiming for all people the good news of Jesus as Lord shook many pillars of Roman power.

This passage parallels the warnings Jesus gives his disciples in Mark: "Watch out for yourselves. They will hand you over to the courts. You will be beaten in synagogues. You will be arraigned before governors and kings because of me, as a witness before them.... But say whatever will be given you at that hour. For it will not be you who are speaking, but the holy Spirit" (13:9–11). The disciples do not witness to Jesus before the hostile world on their own, but through the power of the Advocate. In 15:26 John lays the foundation for future Trinitarian formulations: "When the Advocate comes whom I will send you from the Father, the Spirit of truth that proceeds from the Father, he will testify to me."

Christians sometimes bask in the sunshine of John 3:16 ("For God so loved the world that he gave his only Son, so that everyone who believes in him might not perish but might have eternal life"), which depicts "the world" as God's beloved creation. But passages such as this one recall the dark clouds of opposition and the possibility of hatred. Nevertheless, because the Paraclete is witnessing through them, Christians can speak out with courage and confidence for life and respect for all, even and especially the poorest of the poor, and against the dangers of material possessions.

John 16:4b–33: Jesus' Resurrection Gives His Disciples Joy, Peace, and the Advocate

4b "I did not tell you this from the beginning, because I was with you. 5 But now I am going to the one who sent me, and not one of you asks me, 'Where are you going?' 6 But because I told you this, grief has filled your hearts.

[7] But I tell you the truth, it is better for you that I go. For if I do not go, the Advocate will not come to you. But if I go, I will send him to you. [8] And when he comes he will convict the world in regard to sin and righteousness and condemnation: [9] sin, because they do not believe in me; [10] righteousness, because I am going to the Father and you will no longer see me; [11] condemnation, because the ruler of this world has been condemned.

[12] "I have much more to tell you, but you cannot bear it now. [13] But when he comes, the Spirit of truth, he will guide you to all truth. He will not speak on his own, but he will speak what he hears, and will declare to you the things that are coming. [14] He will glorify me, because he will take from what is mine and declare it to you. [15] Everything that the Father has is mine; for this reason I told you that he will take from what is mine and declare it to you.

[16] "A little while and you will no longer see me, and again a little while later and you will see me." [17] So some of his disciples said to one another, "What does this mean that he is saying to us, 'A little while and you will not see me, and again a little while and you will see me,' and 'Because I am going to the Father'?" [18] So they said, "What is this 'little while' [of which he speaks]? We do not know what he means." [19] Jesus knew that they wanted to ask him, so he said to them, "Are you discussing with one another what I said, 'A little while and you will not see me, and again a little while and you will see me'? [20] Amen, amen, I say to you, you will weep and mourn, while the world rejoices; you will grieve, but your grief will become joy. [21] When a woman is in labor, she is in anguish because her hour has arrived; but when she has given birth to a child, she no longer remembers the pain because of her joy that a child has been born into the world. [22] So you also are now in anguish. But I will see you again, and your hearts will rejoice, and no one will take

your joy away from you. ²³ On that day you will not question me about anything. Amen, amen, I say to you, whatever you ask the Father in my name he will give you. ²⁴ Until now you have not asked anything in my name; ask and you will receive, so that your joy may be complete.

²⁵ "I have told you this in figures of speech. The hour is coming when I will no longer speak to you in figures but I will tell you clearly about the Father. ²⁶ On that day you will ask in my name, and I do not tell you that I will ask the Father for you. ²⁷ For the Father himself loves you, because you have loved me and have come to believe that I came from God. ²⁸ I came from the Father and have come into the world. Now I am leaving the world and going back to the Father." ²⁹ His disciples said, "Now you are talking plainly, and not in any figure of speech. ³⁰ Now we realize that you know everything and that you do not need to have anyone question you. Because of this we believe that you came from God." ³¹ Jesus answered them, "Do you believe now? ³² Behold, the hour is coming and has arrived when each of you will be scattered to his own home and you will leave me alone. But I am not alone, because the Father is with me. ³³ I have told you this so that you might have peace in me. In the world you will have trouble, but take courage, I have conquered the world."

After Jesus' long discourse on the true vine, mutual love, and the world's hatred, the Evangelist returns to themes expressed earlier in 13:31–14:31: Jesus' going away, prayer, the Advocate. He creates a dialogue in which the disciples pose questions that allow Jesus to speak about these subjects. Unlike previous passages, however, the disciples here — as in verses 17–18 and 29–30 — remain unnamed. The key to grasping the many themes in this section of John's Gospel is Jesus' resurrection, which turns the disciples' sorrow into joy, their anxiety into peace, and grants the Holy Spirit. Jesus' words here foreshadow his appearing after "a little while" to the disciples, even though they had locked the doors (see 20:19–23).

John 14:15–17, 25–26 stressed the role of the Advocate in helping the disciples remember and in seeing the deeper meaning of Jesus' identity as the one sent from the Father and of his teaching and signs. Although this passage reiterates that function of the Advocate (13), it places greater emphasis on the Advocate's role as witness, prosecuting attorney, and even judge against the world (5–11). The Advocate will convict the world for not believing in Jesus (sin), for not judging rightly about him (righteousness), and for condemning Jesus to death (condemnation). Indeed, Jesus will not leave his disciples orphans (14:18), but will empower them with the Paraclete to continue his mission.

This Gospel has already stated that the disciples' mission moves forward on the wheels of powerful prayer: "[W]hatever you ask in my name, I will do, so that the Father may be glorified in the Son. If you ask anything of me in my name, I will do it" (14:13–14). This passage restates the theme of prayer, consoling the disciples by telling them that the Father wants to hear their prayers. "[W]hatever you ask the Father in my name he will give you. Until now you have not asked anything in my name; ask and you will receive, so that your joy may be complete…. On that day you will ask in my name, and I do not tell you that I will ask the Father for you. For the Father himself loves you, because you have loved me and have come to believe that I came from God" (16:23–24, 26–27). These assurances reiterate what Jesus previously told his disciples: "On that day you will ask in my name, and I do not tell you that I will ask the Father for you. For the Father himself loves you.... " (16:26–27). They stride along, confident that Jesus has conquered every power that might stand in the way of accomplishing their mission: "In the world you will have trouble, but take courage, I have conquered the world" (16:33).

Perhaps more than the previous sections of Jesus' Farewell Discourse, this passage calls attention to the disciples' sorrow at Jesus' departure. The great loss that is his death will cause them to be scattered (16:32). But disciples, then and now, rest secure in Jesus' promises that he has conquered the world, will turn sorrow into joy and peace, and will send the powerful Paraclete as guide and advocate.

John 17:1–26: Jesus Stands Ever Ready to Intercede for His Present and Future Sheep

¹ When Jesus had said this, he raised his eyes to heaven and said, "Father, the hour has come. Give glory to your son, so that your son may glorify you, ² just as you gave him authority over all people, so that he may give eternal life to all you gave him. ³ Now this is eternal life, that they should know you, the only true God, and the one whom you sent, Jesus Christ. ⁴ I glorified you on earth by accomplishing the work that you gave me to do. ⁵ Now glorify me, Father, with you, with the glory that I had with you before the world began.

⁶ "I revealed your name to those whom you gave me out of the world. They belonged to you, and you gave

them to me, and they have kept your word. 7 Now they know that everything you gave me is from you, 8 because the words you gave to me I have given to them, and they accepted them and truly understood that I came from you, and they have believed that you sent me. 9 I pray for them. I do not pray for the world but for the ones you have given me, because they are yours, 10 and everything of mine is yours and everything of yours is mine, and I have been glorified in them. 11 And now I will no longer be in the world, but they are in the world, while I am coming to you. Holy Father, keep them in your name that you have given me, so that they may be one just as we are. 12 When I was with them I protected them in your name that you gave me, and I guarded them, and none of them was lost except the son of destruction, in order that the scripture might be fulfilled. 13 But now I am coming to you. I speak this in the world so that they may share my joy completely. 14 I gave them your word, and the world hated them, because they do not belong to the world any more than I belong to the world. 15 I do not ask that you take them out of the world but that you keep them from the evil one. 16 They do not belong to the world any more than I belong to the world. 17 Consecrate them in the truth. Your word is truth. 18 As you sent me into the world, so I sent them into the world. 19 And I consecrate myself for them, so that they also may be consecrated in truth.

20 "I pray not only for them, but also for those who will believe in me through their word, 21 so that they may all be one, as you, Father, are in me and I in you, that they also may be in us, that the world may believe that you sent me. 22 And I have given them the glory you gave me, so that they may be one, as we are one, 23 I in them and you in me, that they may be brought to perfection as one, that the world may know that you sent me, and

that you loved them even as you loved me. [24] Father, they are your gift to me. I wish that where I am they also may be with me, that they may see my glory that you gave me, because you loved me before the foundation of the world. [25] Righteous Father, the world also does not know you, but I know you, and they know that you sent me. [26] I made known to them your name and I will make it known, that the love with which you loved me may be in them and I in them."

John's Gospel began with the community's prayer that praised the Word, described the Word's origin and mission, and proclaimed that the Word had become flesh. The community praised God for the abundant grace that the Word had bestowed on them. Their prayer concludes: "No one has ever seen God. The only Son, God, who is at the Father's side, has revealed him" (1:18). As the Word become flesh stands at the brink of his passion and resurrection, he utters a prayer that summarizes his mission. At times it is the prayer of one who is about to die. At other times it is the prayer of one who has already suffered death on the cross and has been glorified, thus the prayer of the exalted Lord for his present and future disciples. Like the Lord's Prayer in Matthew, Jesus' prayer in this passage provides his disciples a blueprint for their prayer. Earlier passages (14:13–14; 15:7–8, 16; 16:23–27) stressed the necessity of prayer. This one provides the content, in the form of several individual petitions.

First, Jesus prays to the Father that he may be glorified: "Give glory to your son, so that your son may glorify you" (1), and "Now glorify me, Father, with you, with the glory that I had with you before the world began" (5). Although Jesus will be vilified through a most shameful

144

and dishonorable death, the Father will raise him up, thus reestablishing his reputation and bestowing on him the greatest honor. Such glorification will also give glory to the Father, whom Jesus represents.

Next, Jesus offers three prayers for his present disciples. "Holy Father, keep them in your name that you have given me, so that they may be one just as we are" (11). After Jesus' death the hostile world will turn against his disciples. Jesus asks that his Father keep them safe through his saving power. Jesus then prays, "I do not ask that you take them out of the world but that you keep them from the evil one" (15). Because the disciples' mission has to be in the world, Jesus prays that his Father preserve them from falling away because of hatred and the enticements of evil. Finally, he prays, "Consecrate them in the truth" (17). This Gospel has reiterated that truth is Jesus' revelation of the Father and that he has come from the Father. This truth makes the disciples holy, set apart from the hostile world that does not want to accept the truth that Jesus is and brings.

The passage concludes with two prayers for future disciples. Jesus asks the Father, "I pray not only for them, but also for those who will believe in me through their word" (20). The disciples go on mission not by their own power but by the power of Jesus, who intercedes for their success. Jesus' final prayer expresses his desire that his disciples join him: "I wish that where I am they also may be with me, that they may see my glory that you gave me, because you loved me before the foundation of the world" (24).

These magnificent words of Jesus are often used in ecumenical contexts, when divided Christians pray that they may be one as the Father and Son are one. But John 17 should be used far more often than once a year during the Week of Church Unity. It is indeed the equivalent of the Lord's Prayer and a summary of what Jesus stood for. Catechists should give this passage the prominence it deserves, because what Jesus prayed two millennia ago he continues to pray even at this moment. Jesus is always interceding for us at the throne of grace. When our discipleship is failing, when our mission is faltering, when the power of evil seems overwhelming, we must look to and rely on Jesus who is praying, lovingly and powerfully, to his Father for us.

VI

Narrative of Jesus' Death, Resurrection Appearances, and Return to the Father (18:1–21:25)

*John 18:1–11: The Noble Shepherd Freely
Hands Himself Over to the Powers of Darkness*

[1] When he had said this, Jesus went out with his disciples across the Kidron valley to where there was a garden, into which he and his disciples entered. [2] Judas his betrayer also knew the place, because Jesus had often met there with his disciples. [3] So Judas got a band of soldiers and guards from the chief priests and the Pharisees and went there with lanterns, torches, and weapons. [4] Jesus, knowing everything that was going to happen to him, went out and said to them, "Whom are you looking for?" [5] They answered him, "Jesus the Nazorean." He said to them, "I AM." Judas his betrayer was also with them. [6] When he said to them, "I AM," they turned away and fell to the ground. [7] So he again asked them, "Whom are you looking for?" They said, "Jesus the Nazorean." [8] Jesus answered, "I told you that I AM. So if you are looking for me, let these men go." [9] This was to fulfill what he had said, "I have not lost any of those you gave me." [10] Then Simon Peter, who had a sword, drew it, struck the high priest's slave, and cut off his right ear. The slave's name was Malchus. [11] Jesus said to Peter, "Put your sword into its scabbard. Shall I not drink the cup that the Father gave me?"

John's version of what happened in the Garden of Gethsemane differs in some respects from the Synoptic versions, especially Mark 14:32–52. Throughout his Farewell Discourse Jesus had been talking about the meaning of his hour, the hour when he would leave this world and return to the Father. That hour has now arrived. But Jesus does not face it with human dread, nor does Judas play a leading role, as recounted in Mark. As the noble shepherd, Jesus freely hands himself over to arrest and subsequently to being lifted up on a cross, so as to draw all people to himself.

With typical irony, John describes Jesus' arrest: "So Judas got a band of soldiers and guards from the chief priests and the Pharisees and went there with lanterns, torches, and weapons" (3). Earlier in this Gospel (7:32), the chief priests and the Pharisees had sent guards to arrest Jesus, but had not succeeded. Now they try again with a "band" of Roman soldiers. While such a "band" might refer to an entire cohort of 480 soldiers, more likely the first "century" of a cohort, eighty men, would have been dispatched for such an errand. They come with lanterns and torches, so that they can light up the garden — and their own darkness — so as see Jesus, the light of the world.

Jesus controls the situation totally; he, the intended arrestee, asks this huge arresting party what they want. Twice he responds with the divine "I AM." The first time Jesus so identifies himself, this mass of armed men falls to the ground in submission to his divine status. After asking again who they had come for and again responding I AM, he allows himself to be apprehended, but only after keeping his disciples free from the powers of darkness. He thus fulfills his role as noble shepherd: "No one can take them [his sheep] out of my hand" (10:28). He also fulfills what he had said to his Father: "I protected them in your name that you gave me, and I guarded them" (17:12).

The Synoptics do not identify the disciple who struck the servant's ear, but John does. Not surprisingly, it is Peter, who had boasted that he would lay down his life for Jesus (13:37). Peter may well represent those disciples who have yet to learn that in Jesus' kingdom, one not of this world, control is not exercised through violence. As Jesus will soon explain to Pilate, "My kingdom does not belong to this world. If my kingdom did belong to this world, my attendants [would] be fighting to keep me from being handed over to the Jews. But as it is, my kingdom is not here" (18:36).

The details of the passion account unique to John reveal an important point of this Gospel. The principal lesson John wants to teach in this passage has already been illustrated in Jesus' washing his disciples' feet. For their sake and for ours, Jesus, the I AM, goes willingly to a most shameful death.

John 18:12–27: Jesus Gives Steadfast Testimony While Peter Falters and Falls

¹² So the band of soldiers, the tribune, and the Jewish guards seized Jesus, bound him, ¹³ and brought him to Annas first. He was the father-in-law of Caiaphas, who was high priest that year. ¹⁴ It was Caiaphas who had counseled the Jews that it was better that one man should die rather than the people.

¹⁵ Simon Peter and another disciple followed Jesus. Now the other disciple was known to the high priest, and

he entered the courtyard of the high priest with Jesus. [16] But Peter stood at the gate outside. So the other disciple, the acquaintance of the high priest, went out and spoke to the gatekeeper and brought Peter in. [17] Then the maid who was the gatekeeper said to Peter, "You are not one of this man's disciples, are you?" He said, "I am not." [18] Now the slaves and the guards were standing around a charcoal fire that they had made, because it was cold, and were warming themselves. Peter was also standing there keeping warm.

[19] The high priest questioned Jesus about his disciples and about his doctrine. [20] Jesus answered him, "I have spoken publicly to the world. I have always taught in a synagogue or in the temple area where all the Jews gather, and in secret I have said nothing. [21] Why ask me? Ask those who heard me what I said to them. They know what I said." [22] When he had said this, one of the temple guards standing there struck Jesus and said, "Is this the way you answer the high priest?" [23] Jesus answered him, "If I have spoken wrongly, testify to the wrong; but if I have spoken rightly, why do you strike me?" [24] Then Annas sent him bound to Caiaphas the high priest.

[25] Now Simon Peter was standing there keeping warm. And they said to him, "You are not one of his disciples, are you?" He denied it and said, "I am not." [26] One of the slaves of the high priest, a relative of the one whose ear Peter had cut off, said, "Didn't I see you in the garden with him?" [27] Again Peter denied it. And immediately the cock crowed.

This passage contains no trial, no witnesses, no condemnation on the part of the religious authorities. In John's narrative all that has taken place earlier, when the Sanhedrin considered what to do with Jesus after the raising of Lazarus, when the high priest, Caiaphas, counseled that "one man should die instead of the people, so that the whole nation may not perish" (see 11:47-50). John notes, "So from that day on they planned to kill him" (11:53). Before Annas, Jesus does not defend himself with new teaching or even clarification of his previous teaching, but by asserting that his teaching was public. He gave his bread of life discourse at the synagogue in Capernaum (6:59), and gave many of his other discourses in the Temple (see 2:13–23; 5:1–41; 7:14–10:39). This passage is significant in that it demonstrates Jesus remaining steadfast in his continued witness.

Unlike Jesus, who remains steadfast, Peter demonstrates his cowardice in the face of three tiny interrogations. The Evangelist further contrasts Peter with Jesus through the literary device of intercalation, that is, creating a verbal "sandwich." Peter's denials (15–18 and 25–27) are the bread. Jesus' unflagging witness to the truth (19–24) is the meat. Peter's lack of resolve is further contrasted with the steadfastness of "the other disciple," probably the Beloved Disciple, who enters the high priest's courtyard with Jesus and eventually follows him to the cross (see 19:25–27). Peter's denials fulfill Jesus' prediction, "Amen, amen, I say to you, the cock will not crow before you deny me three times" (13:38), but they are not the Evangelist's last word about him. After the resurrection, as the Risen Lord Jesus offers forgiveness to his wayward disciple, Peter will counter his threefold denial with a triple confession of his love for Jesus (21:15–17).

John also employs subtle symbolism by noting a charcoal fire burning when Peter denies Jesus (18:18) as well as when Jesus invites his disciples to a post-resurrection meal of reunion (21:9). Even though there is at least one other instance where such a detail would have been reasonable ("The Feast of the Dedication was then taking place in Jerusalem. It was winter" [10:22]), these are the only places in which John's Gospel mentions a charcoal fire. Surely, sword-wielding and master-denying Peter fails here as a disciple, but discipleship does not stop with failure. Jesus' gifts of forgiveness and care for his sheep transform Peter the bungler into Peter the rock.

The Evangelist's portrayal of Jesus and Peter is meant to strengthen disciples who because of their faith in Jesus have to face a trial, whether from "the Jews" or from the Romans. In this section of John's passion account Jesus faces "the Jews." In the next, he must face the Romans.

John 18:28–19:16a: Who Is On Trial? Jesus or Pilate?

28 Then they brought Jesus from Caiaphas to the praetorium. It was morning. And they themselves did not enter the praetorium, in order not to be defiled so that they could eat the Passover. 29 So Pilate came out to them and said, "What charge do you bring [against] this man?" 30 They answered and said to him, "If he were not a criminal, we would not have handed him over to you." 31 At this, Pilate said to them, "Take him yourselves, and judge him according to your law." The Jews answered him, "We do not have the right to execute anyone," 32 in order that the word of Jesus might be fulfilled that he said indicating the kind of death he would die. 33 So Pilate went back into the praetorium and summoned Jesus and said to him, "Are you the King of the Jews?" 34 Jesus answered, "Do you say this on your own or have others told you about me?" 35 Pilate answered, "I am not a Jew, am I? Your own nation and the chief priests handed you over to me. What have

you done?" ³⁶ Jesus answered, "My kingdom does not belong to this world. If my kingdom did belong to this world, my attendants [would] be fighting to keep me from being handed over to the Jews. But as it is, my kingdom is not here." ³⁷ So Pilate said to him, "Then you are a king?" Jesus answered, "You say I am a king. For this I was born and for this I came into the world, to testify to the truth. Everyone who belongs to the truth listens to my voice." ³⁸ Pilate said to him, "What is truth?"

When he had said this, he again went out to the Jews and said to them, "I find no guilt in him. ³⁹ But you have a custom that I release one prisoner to you at Passover. Do you want me to release to you the King of the Jews?" ⁴⁰ They cried out again, "Not this one but Barabbas!" Now Barabbas was a revolutionary.

¹⁹:¹ Then Pilate took Jesus and had him scourged. ² And the soldiers wove a crown out of thorns and placed it on his head, and clothed him in a purple cloak, ³ and they came to him and said, "Hail, King of the Jews!" And they struck him repeatedly. ⁴ Once more Pilate went out and said to them, "Look, I am bringing him out to you, so that you may know that I find no guilt in him." ⁵ So Jesus came out, wearing the crown of thorns and the purple cloak. And he said to them, "Behold, the man!" ⁶ When the chief priests and the guards saw him they cried out, "Crucify him, crucify him!" Pilate said to them, "Take him yourselves and crucify him. I find no guilt in him." ⁷ The Jews answered, "We have a law, and according to that law he ought to die, because he made himself the Son of God." ⁸ Now when Pilate heard this statement, he became even more afraid, ⁹ and went back into the praetorium and said to Jesus, "Where are you from?" Jesus did not answer him. ¹⁰ So Pilate said to him, "Do you not speak to me? Do you not know that I have power to release you and I have power to crucify you?" ¹¹ Jesus answered [him], "You

would have no power over me if it had not been given to you from above. For this reason the one who handed me over to you has the greater sin." 12 Consequently, Pilate tried to release him; but the Jews cried out, "If you release him, you are not a Friend of Caesar. Everyone who makes himself a king opposes Caesar."

13 When Pilate heard these words he brought Jesus out and seated him on the judge's bench in the place called Stone Pavement, in Hebrew, Gabbatha. 14 It was preparation day for Passover, and it was about noon. And he said to the Jews, "Behold, your king!" 15 They cried out, "Take him away, take him away! Crucify him!" Pilate said to them, "Shall I crucify your king?" The chief priests answered, "We have no king but Caesar." 16a Then he handed him over to them to be crucified.

John's account of Jesus' trial before Pilate is longer than comparable accounts in the Synoptics and, in typical Johannine fashion, uses irony liberally to convey its message. The readers of this Gospel know that Jesus is the Son of God, sent from the Father for the life of the world. They also know that the world, that is, human beings turned in upon themselves and hostile to God, rejects Jesus and his teaching. In the figures of the religious authorities and Pilate, this passage shows the powers of the world arrayed against Jesus. John intends that his readers also keep in mind that Pilate represented the most powerful nation of that age, whose emperors had brought peace to the world but maintained that peace with savage force. The seven scenes that comprise this trial are shot through with irony as Pilate moves inside and outside the praetorium.

The opening exchange (18:28–32) contains the first of many taunts with which Pilate underlines Jewish submission to the might of Rome, for the subservient Jewish authorities do not have the right to execute anyone. These verses contain two ironic statements. The religious authorities do not want to pollute themselves ritually by stepping on Gentile soil, yet they will morally pollute themselves at the end of the trial when they deny their King and God and confess: "We have no king but Caesar" (19:15). Thrice before in predicting Jesus' death the Evangelist had described it as being lifted up (3:14; 8:28; 12:32). Of those, 12:32 is especially significant: "And when I am lifted up from the earth, I will draw everyone to myself."

In verses 33 to 38a Pilate interrogates Jesus, who answers his question about kingship by redirecting it from political terms and the use of violence. From the beginning, John's Gospel has shown that Jesus is full of "grace and truth" (1:14, 17). This is not the mathematical truth that $2 + 2 = 4$, but the truth that is God and that has been revealed in and through Jesus, who is "the way and the truth and the life" (14:6). When Pilate asks "What is truth?" it is clear that he does not belong to the truth, is not on God's side, is not listening to the truth standing right before him.

Pilate then moves again from Jesus to address the Jews (38b–40). For the first time Pilate proclaims Jesus' innocence. Passover celebrated God's liberation of the chosen people. In commemoration of that feast the religious authorities want Pilate to set free not Jesus, their king, but a violent revolutionary. They want Barabbas ("son of the father") rather than Jesus, Son of the Father.

Pilate returns to the praetorium (19:1–3) and orders something that seems contrary to procedure, for scourging

155

and attendant mockery usually take place after condemnation. But the Evangelist is not concerned with portraying the Roman legal system. By placing the scourging and mockery here, he puts them at the center of his theological narrative. Three scenes lead up to this passage, and three follow it. While the emperor might wear a crown of gold and be clothed in royal purple, Jesus is given a crown of thorns and the soldiers' cheap purple clothing. Ironically, their mockery, "Hail, King of the Jews," conveys the truth. From the cross, Jesus is King.

Then Pilate presents Jesus, crowned and cloaked as king, to the religious authorities and declares twice that he finds Jesus innocent (19:4–7). As he does so, he makes a puzzling statement: "Behold, the man!" In the context of this Gospel's dramatic theology, his declaration has to have a more profound meaning than "Here's the guy you handed over to me!" A parallel statement from the First Book of Samuel that tells of God's appointment through Samuel of Saul as the first king of Israel provides a context for Pilate's pronouncement. Concerning Saul, the Lord says to Samuel: "Behold the man" (9:17*). In response, the religious authorities switch from making the political accusation that Jesus pretended to be a king to bringing a religious charge against him: "[H]e made himself the Son of God" (19:7). John's readers know that Jesus didn't make himself the Son of God. He was the Son of God.

In response, a dumbfounded Pilate asks a question that the Evangelist has tried to answer time and time again: "Where are you from?" (19:8). Readers know that Jesus is from God, the one God sent. Jesus does not answer Pilate's question, but instead raises his own: "You would have no power over me if it had not been given to you from

156

above." (19:11). Who has ultimate power? Certainly not all-powerful Rome.

Pilate's next actions are filled with irony. Pilate seats Jesus on the judgment bench. Perhaps Pilate, the judge, does this to mock Jesus. For the Evangelist, however, Jesus is the true judge at this trial. The religious leaders don't want Jesus as king and, on the preparation day for Passover, defile themselves by declaring that the king to whom they pledge allegiance is no longer God, but Caesar. Jesus judges them too.

John's Gospel has presented one representative figure after another. This passage offers a negative representative character, Pilate. Thrice he declares Jesus innocent. Twice he tries to dialogue with Jesus, but his ears are insufficiently trained to hear the Truth. He plays political games with the religious authorities, whom he loves to taunt. In the end, however, these religious authorities play the trump card: If Pilate lets a pretender king go free, then he has betrayed Caesar, an error that could cost him his position and perhaps his life. Does Pilate represent the powers of the world who will be interrogating disciples about their faith? Or does he represent those who are wishy-washy in the face of Jesus?

*John 19:16b–37: Jesus, the Crucified King,
Willingly and Lovingly Gives Up His Life*

> [16b] So they took Jesus, [17] and carrying the cross himself he went out to what is called the Place of the Skull, in Hebrew, Golgotha. [18] There they crucified him, and with him two others, one on either side, with Jesus in the middle. [19] Pilate also had an inscription written and put on the cross. It read, "Jesus the Nazorean, the King of

157

the Jews." ²⁰ Now many of the Jews read this inscription, because the place where Jesus was crucified was near the city; and it was written in Hebrew, Latin, and Greek. ²¹ So the chief priests of the Jews said to Pilate, "Do not write 'The King of the Jews,' but that he said, 'I am the King of the Jews.' " ²² Pilate answered, "What I have written, I have written."

²³ When the soldiers had crucified Jesus, they took his clothes and divided them into four shares, a share for each soldier. They also took his tunic, but the tunic was seamless, woven in one piece from the top down. ²⁴ So they said to one another, "Let's not tear it, but cast lots for it to see whose it will be," in order that the passage of scripture might be fulfilled [that says]: "They divided my garments among them, and for my vesture they cast lots." This is what the soldiers did. ²⁵ Standing by the cross of Jesus were his mother and his mother's sister, Mary the wife of Clopas, and Mary of Magdala. ²⁶ When Jesus saw his mother and the disciple there whom he loved, he said to his mother, "Woman, behold, your son." ²⁷ Then he said to the disciple, "Behold, your mother." And from that hour the disciple took her into his home.

²⁸ After this, aware that everything was now finished, in order that the scripture might be fulfilled, Jesus said, "I thirst." ²⁹ There was a vessel filled with common wine. So they put a sponge soaked in wine on a sprig of hyssop and put it up to his mouth. ³⁰ When Jesus had taken the wine, he said, "It is finished." And bowing his head, he handed over the spirit.

³¹ Now since it was preparation day, in order that the bodies might not remain on the cross on the sabbath, for the sabbath day of that week was a solemn one, the Jews asked Pilate that their legs be broken and they be taken down. ³² So the soldiers came and broke the legs of the first and then of the other one who was crucified with Jesus. ³³ But when they came to Jesus and saw that he was already dead, they did not break his legs, ³⁴ but one

soldier thrust his lance into his side, and immediately blood and water flowed out. [35] An eyewitness has testified, and his testimony is true; he knows that he is speaking the truth, so that you also may [come to] believe. [36] For this happened so that the scripture passage might be fulfilled: "Not a bone of it will be broken." [37] And again another passage says: "They will look upon him whom they have pierced."

John's account of Jesus' crucifixion leaves out characters and incidents that the Synoptics include. There is no Simon of Cyrene, because Jesus, the noble shepherd, freely, on his own, gives up his life. There are no religious authorities to mock and taunt Jesus. There is no Roman centurion who speaks about the significance of Jesus' death on the cross. No earthquake shakes Jerusalem nor does darkness fall at midday. The thieves crucified with Jesus do not speak, either in taunt or in petition. Jesus himself does not pray a psalm of desolation.

Jesus' crucifixion had been predicted. As the early Church recited Jesus' salvific death as part of its creed, it declared that he died in accordance with the Scriptures. The soldiers divide Jesus' clothing in accordance with the Scriptures. His death by crucifixion alone and not by having his legs broken is also in accordance with the Scriptures. He has willingly completed the work the Father has given him in accordance with the Scriptures.

Besides this theme of fulfilling Scripture, the Gospel of John has other emphases. Jesus dies at the time when Passover lambs are being slaughtered. He indeed is the Lamb of God who takes away the sin of the world (1:29). The inscription over the cross proclaims in three languages the universality of salvation in Jesus. Now that he is lifted up, he draws all people to himself. Jesus names the Beloved Disciple as his successor and gives his Mother into the disciple's care, thus forming a new community of believers. For her part Jesus' Mother, who first appeared at the wedding Feast in Cana (2:1–11), remains faithful to her son; she represents those who wait patiently and find salvation in Jesus of Nazareth.

From Jesus' pierced side flow blood and water, the two elements essential to life. Thus what Jesus taught about those who eat his flesh and drink his blood having eternal life (6:52–57) and about his providing rivers of living water (7:38) has come true: he gives the blood and the water of life to those who believe in him.

The Beloved Disciple is not only Jesus' successor, but also the solemn witness to the saving significance of Jesus' death on the cross: "An eyewitness has testified, and his testimony is true; he knows that he is speaking the truth, so that you also may [come to] believe" (35). Using legal terminology such as "eyewitness" and "testimony" recalls the trials that Jesus has endured throughout his ministry. Now as the verdict of Pilate and the religious authorities is being played out — that Jesus is worthy of death — God utters a different verdict about his Son: from the cross Jesus reigns as King and bestows life.

In my Franciscan tradition the San Damiano cross, a Byzantine cross inspired by John's Gospel, is very important. The Christ depicted on it is not a brutalized crucified Christ, but the serene crucified Christ from whose side water and blood flow to nourish the faithful who stand beneath. John's account of Jesus' death is powerfully different from the Synoptic accounts as it underscores not what humans have done to God's Son, but what God's Son has done for humankind.

John 19:38–42: Nicodemus, Drawn to Jesus, Gives Him a Royal Burial

[38] After this, Joseph of Arimathea, secretly a disciple of Jesus for fear of the Jews, asked Pilate if he could remove the body of Jesus. And Pilate permitted it. So he came and took his body. [39] Nicodemus, the one who had first come to him at night, also came bringing a mixture of myrrh and aloes weighing about one hundred pounds. [40] They took the body of Jesus and bound it with burial cloths along with the spices, according to the Jewish burial custom. [41] Now in the place where he had been crucified there was a garden, and in the garden a new tomb, in which no one had yet been buried. [42] So they laid Jesus there because of the Jewish preparation day; for the tomb was close by.

It is tempting to skim past this passage to get to the account of Jesus' resurrection, but John's Gospel offers it as a moment to pause and reflect. Only John mentions Nicodemus. Perhaps since his first appearance early in this Gospel, Nicodemus has been searching for Jesus, or rather, Jesus has been searching for him. At night Nicodemus, a member of Jesus' opposition, had come to him for enlightenment (3:1–15). When his fellow religious leaders were on the verge of condemning Jesus, Nicodemus stood up for him (7:50–52). Now after Jesus' death the Evangelist links Nicodemus with Joseph of Arimathea, whose name and deeds are set deep within the gospel tradition. Nicodemus is a prime example of the power of Jesus' exaltation on the cross: "And when I am lifted up from the earth, I will draw everyone to myself" (12:32).

Nicodemus, a member of the group responsible for Jesus' death, has become one of his disciples. One who would confine Jesus to the margins of society has become an insider.

Nicodemus must have been wealthy; he brings one hundred Roman pounds of spices, the equivalent of seventy-five pounds in contemporary measures. If the twelve ounces of nard Mary used to anoint Jesus' feet was worth 300 days' wages (see 12:5), imagine the value of seventy-five pounds of spices. This vast amount may also suggest the royal nature of Jesus' burial; Josephus, the Jewish historian, notes that at the burial of King Herod the Great, five hundred servants bore spices.

Within the Johannine community stands one who had been an enemy, but who kept seeking, never turning his back completely on the truth and light. In the end he found the light, one of the first to be given life by the water and blood that flowed from Jesus' pierced side.

John 20:1–18: Mary of Magdala and the Beloved Disciple Are the First to Believe

[1] On the first day of the week, Mary of Magdala came to the tomb early in the morning, while it was still dark, and saw the stone removed from the tomb. [2] So she ran and went to Simon Peter and to the other disciple whom Jesus loved, and told them, "They have taken the Lord from the tomb, and we don't know where they put him." [3] So Peter and the other disciple went out and came to the tomb. [4] They both ran, but the other disciple ran faster than Peter and arrived at the tomb first; [5] he bent down and saw the burial cloths there, but did not go in. [6] When Simon Peter arrived after him, he went into the tomb and saw the burial cloths there, [7] and the cloth that had cov-

ered his head, not with the burial cloths but rolled up in a separate place. [8] Then the other disciple also went in, the one who had arrived at the tomb first, and he saw and believed. [9] For they did not yet understand the scripture that he had to rise from the dead. [10] Then the disciples returned home.

[11] But Mary stayed outside the tomb weeping. And as she wept, she bent over into the tomb [12] and saw two angels in white sitting there, one at the head and one at the feet where the body of Jesus had been. [13] And they said to her, "Woman, why are you weeping?" She said to them, "They have taken my Lord, and I don't know where they laid him." [14] When she had said this, she turned around and saw Jesus there, but did not know it was Jesus. [15] Jesus said to her, "Woman, why are you weeping? Whom are you looking for?" She thought it was the gardener and said to him, "Sir, if you carried him away, tell me where you laid him, and I will take him." [16] Jesus said to her, "Mary!" She turned and said to him in Hebrew, "Rabbouni," which means Teacher. [17] Jesus said to her, "Stop holding on to me, for I have not yet ascended to the Father. But go to my brothers and tell them, 'I am going to my Father and your Father, to my God and your God.' " [18] Mary of Magdala went and announced to the disciples, "I have seen the Lord," and what he told her.

In a successful joke, that briefest of narratives, the punch line or ending brings the entire story together. In explaining this Gospel, too, homilists must not forget the basic principle of narrative: a story hangs from its ending. This passage, the beginning of the conclusion to the Gospel, refers back to earlier parts of the narrative. It has three main characters: Peter, the Beloved Disciple, and Mary of Magdala.

In his farewell discourse Jesus reiterated to his disciples that after his death, resurrection, and ascension their sorrow would be turned to joy. For example, in 16:20 he says, "Amen, amen, I say to you, you will weep and mourn, while the world rejoices; you will grieve, but your grief will become joy." The burial cloths that the two disciples find were foreshadowed in the story of Jesus' raising of Lazarus: "The dead man came out, tied hand and foot with burial bands, and his face was wrapped in a cloth. So Jesus said to them, 'Untie him and let him go' " (11:44). The risen Lord Jesus does not need anyone to untie his burial garments, which are not cast aside haphazardly but folded neatly. Death has not held him bound, for the noble shepherd does what he does freely: "No one takes it [my life] from me, but I lay it down on my own. I have power to lay it down, and power to take it up again" (10:18). Jesus' sheep " ... hear his voice, as he calls his own sheep by name and leads them out" (10:3). When Jesus calls Mary by name, she recognizes her teacher, her Rabbouni. Jesus asked his first disciples: "What are you looking for?" (1:38). He repeats that question to Mary of Magdala: "Whom are you looking for?" (20:15). The Evangelist mentioned Mary of Magdala for the first time when she was at the cross with the other faithful followers of Jesus, his Mother and the Beloved Disciple (19:26). Now, at the sight of the glorified Jesus, her grief and sorrow turn into joy.

Whenever this Gospel has paired the two, the Beloved Disciple has bested Peter. At the Last Supper Peter has to ask the Beloved Disciple who Jesus' betrayer is. The Beloved Disciple is the one who gets Peter into the court-yard of the high priest. Now, the Beloved Disciple out-races Peter to the empty tomb, and believes. In the next chapter (21:1–14) the Beloved Disciple, not Peter, recognizes the risen Lord Jesus. Although steadfast as a disciple, Peter's faith is still limited. On the other hand, with the insight of faith the Beloved Disciple can infer from the neatly separated and folded burial cloths that Jesus has left death behind and has accomplished what he had said in his farewell discourses again and again: He has gone to the Father.

Just as the women in Matthew 28:9 grasp Jesus' feet, Mary, too, tries to hold onto the risen Jesus. But Jesus is in transition to his ascension and gives Mary the commission to go to the other disciples and proclaim: "I am going to my Father and your Father, to my God and your God" (20:17). Mary of Magdala must have been very important in the Johannine community, for she — not Nathanael or Philip or Andrew — gets her own story of how the risen Lord Jesus appeared to her. It is important to note that nowhere in John's Gospel is Mary of Magdala called a sinner. St. Augustine was correct in calling her "the apostle to the apostles." She and the Beloved Disciple are the first to believe in the risen Lord Jesus. Peter's turn will come in the next chapter.

John 20:19–31: Thomas Moves from Unbelief to Belief

19 On the evening of that first day of the week, when the doors were locked, where the disciples were, for fear of the Jews, Jesus came and stood in their midst and said to them, "Peace be with you." 20 When he had said this, he showed them his hands and his side. The disciples rejoiced when they saw the Lord. 21 [Jesus] said to them again, "Peace be with you. As the Father has sent me,

so I send you." ²² And when he had said this, he breathed on them and said to them, "Receive the holy Spirit. ²³ Whose sins you forgive are forgiven them, and whose sins you retain are retained."

²⁴ Thomas, called Didymus, one of the Twelve, was not with them when Jesus came. ²⁵ So the other disciples said to him, "We have seen the Lord." But he said to them, "Unless I see the mark of the nails in his hands and put my finger into the nailmarks and put my hand into his side, I will not believe." ²⁶ Now a week later his disciples were again inside and Thomas was with them. Jesus came, although the doors were locked, and stood in their midst and said, "Peace be with you." ²⁷ Then he said to Thomas, "Put your finger here and see my hands, and bring your hand and put it into my side, and do not be unbelieving, but believe." ²⁸ Thomas answered and said to him, "My Lord and my God!" ²⁹ Jesus said to him, "Have you come to believe because you have seen me? Blessed are those who have not seen and have believed."

³⁰ Now Jesus did many other signs in the presence of [his] disciples that are not written in this book. ³¹ But these are written that you may [come to] believe that Jesus is the Messiah, the Son of God, and that through this belief you may have life in his name.

The Evangelist describes "the disciples"— he does not say how many — gathered in fear behind locked doors, but these locked doors do not prevent Jesus from entering their midst.

Twice he gives them the gift of peace that he had promised in his farewell discourse: "Peace I leave with you; my peace I give to you. Not as the world gives do I give it to you. Do not let your hearts be troubled or afraid" (14:27). Now that Jesus has gone away and come back, he turns their sorrow into rejoicing. In 16:20 he told them: "Amen, amen, I say to you, you will weep and mourn, while the world rejoices; you will grieve, but your grief will become joy." In his final prayer he prayed: "... not only for them, but also for those who will believe in me through their word" (17:20). Having risen and ascended to the Father, Jesus sends his disciples forth to turn the world from sin and death to faith and life.

Throughout Jesus' farewell discourse he had promised his disciples that he would send them the Holy Spirit. Now he breathes that Spirit into them. The Greek word for "breathes" the Evangelist uses here is the same as in the Genesis account (2:7) of creation. As John the Witness said at the beginning of the Gospel, Jesus was to give the Holy Spirit (1:33). On the Jewish Feast of Tabernacles Jesus had talked about his gift of living water, and the Evangelist observed: "He said this in reference to the Spirit that those who came to believe in him were to receive. There was, of course, no Spirit yet, because Jesus had not yet been glorified" (7:39). Now that Jesus has been glorified, he sends the Holy Spirit for the forgiveness of sins.

In his glorified state Jesus' pierced hands and side have special significance. The Jesus who stands before the disciples is the same Jesus who journeyed with them in Galilee and Judea, but from his wounded side have flowed the blood and water of life. His wounds are proof positive of his continued gift of life.

Jesus' key words to Thomas are: "Do not be unbelieving, but believe" (20:27). Thomas is not a doubting Thomas, but an unbelieving Thomas. Just as his fellow disciples did not believe the testimony of Mary of Magdala, so too he doesn't believe the testimony of his fellow disciples. Caravaggio's famous painting shows him putting his finger into Jesus' side, but the Evangelist does not describe Thomas doing so. At the sight of the risen Jesus he is able to move from unbelief to belief in the testimony of his fellow disciples, the same testimony that all future believers will receive. To confess his personal faith in Jesus, Thomas pronounces the same words that the Roman Emperor Domitian required of his subjects: "My Lord and my God."

In his commentary on John's Gospel, St. Bonaventure tells the story of a general whose aide noticed the ugly scars on his body from arrows, spears, and swords. The aide said that they had found a skillful surgeon who could remove them. To this suggestion the general replied: "No, let them be as a sign to my soldiers that I am one of them and go into the heat of battle with them. Let my scars continue to be a sign of my love for my troops." The risen and ascended Lord Jesus will never have his wounds covered over, for they show that the Word who became flesh loved his own until the end.

The Evangelist wrote his Gospel to bolster the faith of those who would read it. In the last two verses of this passage, he states that intention. John's opening verses, the prayer of his Prologue, state who Jesus was and what was in store for him. As it has progressed, to challenge and deepen readers' faith, John's narrative has offered representative characters such as Nicodemus, the Samaritan woman, and the man born blind. We know in faith that we continue to find life in the risen Jesus, one of us.

John 21:1–14: The Risen Lord Jesus Feeds His Disciples Abundantly

[1] After this, Jesus revealed himself again to his disciples at the Sea of Tiberias. He revealed himself in this way. [2] Together were Simon Peter, Thomas called Didymus, Nathanael from Cana in Galilee, Zebedee's sons, and two others of his disciples. [3] Simon Peter said to them, "I am going fishing." They said to him, "We also will come with you." So they went out and got into the boat, but that night they caught nothing. [4] When it was already dawn, Jesus was standing on the shore; but the disciples did not realize that it was Jesus. [5] Jesus said to them, "Children, have you caught anything to eat?" They answered him, "No." [6] So he said to them, "Cast the net over the right side of the boat and you will find something." So they cast it, and were not able to pull it in because of the number of fish. [7] So the disciple whom Jesus loved said to Peter, "It is the Lord." When Simon Peter heard that it was the Lord, he tucked in his garment, for he was lightly clad, and jumped into the sea. [8] The other disciples came in the boat, for they were not far from shore, only about a hundred yards, dragging the net with the fish. [9] When they climbed out on shore, they saw a charcoal fire with fish on it and bread. [10] Jesus said to them, "Bring some of the fish you just caught." [11] So Simon Peter went over and dragged the net ashore full of one hundred fifty-three large fish. Even though there were so many, the net was not torn. [12] Jesus said to them, "Come, have breakfast." And none of the disciples dared to ask him, "Who are you?" because they realized it was the Lord. [13] Jesus came over and took the bread and gave it to them, and in like manner the fish. [14] This was now the third time Jesus was revealed to his disciples after being raised from the dead.

This dramatic story has several strange details. At the beginning of his Gospel, the Evangelist did not describe any of the first disciples who followed Jesus as fishermen. He seemed to have concluded his account with the appearance of the risen Jesus in Jerusalem (20:20–31). Now Jesus appears in Galilee. In his earlier appearance (20:18–24) he had commissioned his disciples to continue his mission to the world; the story in this passage suggests that these privileged disciples turned a deaf ear to that commission and returned to their former way of life. Finally, it would seem logical that having seen the risen Lord on two previous occasions the disciples would recognize him when he appears again. Perhaps, the best explanation for the strange features of this passage is to see all of John 21 as the work of the final editor of the Gospel. This does not mean that John 21 is not canonical or that it is missing in any of the best Greek manuscripts of John, but that, as other details have also suggested, John's Gospel has gone through stages of composition.

As a drama, it should be read on two levels. On the surface level it's a great fish story, but on a deeper level this passage gives narrative expression to Jesus' earlier commission to his disciples: "As the Father has sent me, so I send you" (20:21). But only with Jesus' help can these disciples, who have previously caught nothing, be successful on mission. Obviously, this story uses number symbolism. Seven is the number of completion or perfection, so these seven disciples who go fishing stand for all disciples. Their net contains 153 fish and does not tear. These two details suggest universality and completion, for nothing escapes from the net. That is, all are called. Turning to what is happening on shore, the Evangelist could have merely noted that a fire was burning, but his reference to "a charcoal fire" links this scene to that of Peter's denial of Jesus, where a charcoal fire also was burning (18:18). In the final lines of this passage, when Jesus rehabilitates Peter, the Evangelist again contrasts the beloved disciple with Peter. Peter gets to haul in the net, but the beloved disciple is the first to recognize the presence and work of the risen Lord.

The great fish story conveys the true mission of disciples. In the last two verses (12–13), however, the passage turns into a story about a meal. Just like the two disciples on the way to Emmaus (Lk 24:13–35), the seven disciples recognize Jesus while being fed. In his first sign at Cana Jesus' supplying superabundant wine indicates his gift of life. When he multiplied the five barley loaves and a few fish for five thousand, there were twelve baskets of leftovers. Now he supplies his disciples with another abundant meal. Truly, Jesus is the one who gives life, and isn't it significant that in a fish story like this the Evangelist stresses first that Jesus took the bread and gave it to his disciples, and then the fish? Jesus continues to give his disciples life in the Eucharist.

John 21:15–25: The Last Words about Peter and the Beloved Disciple

15 When they had finished breakfast, Jesus said to Simon Peter, "Simon, son of John, do you love me more than these?" He said to him, "Yes, Lord, you know that I love you." He said to him, "Feed my lambs." 16 He then said to him a second time, "Simon, son of John, do you love me?" He said to him, "Yes, Lord, you know that I love you." He said to him, "Tend my sheep." 17 He said to him the third

time, "Simon, son of John, do you love me?" Peter was distressed that he had said to him a third time, "Do you love me?" and he said to him, "Lord, you know everything; you know that I love you." [Jesus] said to him, "Feed my sheep. 18 Amen, amen, I say to you, when you were younger, you used to dress yourself and go where you wanted; but when you grow old, you will stretch out your hands, and someone else will dress you and lead you where you do not want to go." 19 He said this signifying by what kind of death he would glorify God. And when he had said this, he said to him, "Follow me."

20 Peter turned and saw the disciple following whom Jesus loved, the one who had also reclined upon his chest during the supper and had said, "Master, who is the one who will betray you?" 21 When Peter saw him, he said to Jesus, "Lord, what about him?" 22 Jesus said to him, "What if I want him to remain until I come? What concern is it of yours? You follow me." 23 So the word spread among the brothers that that disciple would not die. But Jesus had not told him that he would not die, just "What if I want him to remain until I come? [What concern is it of yours?]"

24 It is this disciple who testifies to these things and has written them, and we know that his testimony is true. 25 There are also many other things that Jesus did, but if these were to be described individually, I do not think the whole world would contain the books that would be written.

Since chapter 13, the Gospel of John has narrated a succession of Peter's failures. First he doesn't want to get his feet washed. Then he boasts that he will die for Jesus, but at interrogations around a charcoal fire he denies his Master. During the crucifixion he vanishes. He was the first to enter the empty tomb, but he doesn't believe. He is so engrossed in his wondrous catch of fish that he doesn't recognize the one responsible for this largess. This same portion of John's Gospel has noted the devotedness of the Beloved Disciple. At the Last Supper he has the prime place at Jesus' breast, and Peter must ask him who the betrayer might be. He has the influence to let Peter into the courtyard of the high priest. At the cross the Beloved Disciple becomes Jesus' successor, and at the empty tomb he believes that his Master has risen. When Jesus empowers the disciples-turned-fishermen to catch 153 large fish, it is he who recognizes Jesus. In this passage these two complementary disciples make their final appearances.

With the charcoal fire still burning, the risen Jesus offers Peter forgiveness and commissions him as sub-shepherd. Peter's three denials now stand in contrast with his triple confession of love. Jesus commissions him to feed his sheep, that is, as a sub-shepherd, to care for his disciples. Earlier, Jesus said clearly, "A good shepherd lays down his life for the sheep" (10:11). Like his Master, Peter will glorify God through his death by crucifixion. Despite his great office as sub-shepherd of Jesus, Peter must never forget that he remains a disciple of Jesus who has been given the charge: "Follow me" (21:19).

The Beloved Disciple and his witness stand behind the Fourth Gospel. Although the Beloved Disciple may not have been martyred as Peter was, the "we" of the Johannine community treasure him and his witness because he was able to see deeper and more quickly into the identity of Jesus, the Word made flesh, thus imitating his Master who was the exegete of his Father: "No one has ever seen God. The only Son, God, who is at the Father's side, has revealed him" (1:18).

At the end of this extraordinary Gospel it is clear that if we "Let John be John," we can begin to appreciate how John's Gospel builds up our faith. Jesus is presented as our bread of life, our living water, our noble shepherd, our vine, our light, our resurrection and life. We can find ourselves in the representative characters of the Gospel as we search for Jesus with Nicodemus, seek for true light with the man born blind, petition for living water with the Samaritan woman, and persevere in the quest for Jesus with Mary of Magdala. If John's Gospel has brightened your own faith life through your reading and meditation, share the experience with others. Be like the Samaritan woman and tell all and sundry what Jesus has done for you.

Select Bibliography

Brown, Raymond E. *A Retreat with John the Evangelist: That You May Have Life*. Cincinnati: St. Anthony Messenger Press, 1998.

___. *The Gospel According to John (I-XII; XIII-XXI)*. Garden City: Doubleday, 1966, 1970.

Bultmann, Rudolf. *The Gospel of John: A Commentary*. Oxford: Blackwell, 1971.

Carter, Warren. *John: Storyteller, Interpreter, Evangelist*. Peabody, MA: Hendrickson, 2006.

Karris, Robert J. *Jesus and the Marginalized in John's Gospel*. Collegeville: Liturgical Press, 1990.

___. *Prayer and the New Testament: Jesus and His Communities at Worship*. New York: Crossroad, 2000, pp. 82–113.

Kysar, Robert. *Preaching John*. Minneapolis: Fortress, 2002.

Lincoln, Andrew T. *The Gospel According to St John*. Peabody, MA: Hendrickson, 2005.

Lindars, Barnabas. *The Gospel of John*. London: Oliphants, 1972.

Neyrey, Jerome H. *The Gospel of John*. New York: Cambridge University Press, 2007.

Segovia, Fernando F. "The Journey(s) of the Word of God: A Reading of the Plot of the Fourth Gospel," in *The Fourth Gospel from a Literary Perspective*. Semeia 53 (1991), 23–54.

Yee, Gale A. *Jewish Feasts and the Gospel of John*. Wilmington, DE: Michael Glazier, 1989.

In the Same Series from New City Press

Mark
From Death to Life
Dennis Sweetland
ISBN 1-56548-117-8, paper, 5 3/8 x 8 1/2, 216 pp.

Matthew
God With Us
Ronald D. Witherup
ISBN 1-56548-123-2, paper, 5 3/8 x 8 1/2, 216 pp.

Luke
Stories of Joy and Salvation
John Gillman
ISBN 1-56548-173-9, paper, 5 3/8 x 8 1/2, 216 pp.

Paul's Prison Letters
*Scriptural Commentaries on Paul's Letters to Philemon,
the Philippians, and the Colossians*
Daniel Harrington
ISBN 1-56548-088-0, paper, 5 3/8 x 8 1/2, 136 pp.

Revelation
The Book of the Risen Christ
Daniel Harrington
ISBN 1-56548-121-6, paper, 5 3/8 x 8 1/2, 168 pp.

Song of Songs
The Love Poetry of Scripture
Dianne Bergant
ISBN 1-56548-100-3, paper, 5 3/8 x 8 1/2, 168 pp.

To Order:
Phone 1-800-462-5980
www.newcitypress.com